OSHO

Zen

AND

THE ART OF MEDITATION

TALKS ON ZEN BUDDHISM

COLLECTION OF DISCOURSES 1 TO 6 FROM THE BOOK
'TAKE IT EASY, VOL II' BASED ON THE DOKA OF ZEN MASTER IKKYU

Bhagwan Shree Rajneesh
is now known simply
as Osho.
Osho has explained that
His name is derived
from William James' word
'oceanic' which means
dissolving into the ocean.
Oceanic describes the
experience, He says,
but what about the experiencer?
For that we use the word 'Osho'.
Later He came to find out
that 'Osho' has also been
used historically in the
Far East meaning
"The Blessed One, on whom the Sky
Showers Flowers."

OSHO

ZEN
AND
THE ART OF MEDITATION

ISBN 81-7182-501-X

Editing by	:	Ma Ananda Vandana
Design & Coordination by	:	Swami Amano Surdham
Phototypesetting by	:	Tao Publishing Pvt. Ltd., 50, Koregaon , Park, Pune-411001
Publisheed By	:	**Diamond Pocket Books (Pvt.) Ltd.** X-30, Okhla Industrial Area, Phase-II, New Delhi - 110020 Ph. 6841033, 6822803, 6822804 Fax :011-6925020
E-mail	:	mverma@nde.vsnl.net.in
Website	:	www.diamondpocketbooks.com
Edition	:	2000
Price		RS 297 -
Printed at		......nters, Shahdara, Delhi-32

Acknowledgment is given to 'Zen and Zen Classics volumes I and V' by: R. H. Blyth – Hokuseido Press for the doka of Ikkyu quoted in this book.

CONTENTS

FOREWORD

RELAXED ALERTNESS: These two words look diametrically opposite. They are—because whenever you are relaxed you lose alertness, and whenever you are alert you lose relaxedness. And unless they both happen together you will go on missing Buddha's message. Buddha wants you to bring these polarities together. It is the highest synthesis of human consciousness: one polarity is relaxedness, another polarity is alertness.

In the west, attentiveness has been cultivated. The whole educational mechanism forces you to become more attentive. But it tires you, it drives you neurotic, madness becomes a natural by-product of it.

In the East, people have remained in the relaxed state. But if you are relaxed without being attentive, it becomes lethargy, passivity, dullness. Hence the east has remained poor, unscientific, non-technological, starving.

If Buddha's message is rightly understood, there will be meeting of East and West. In Buddha, both can meet. His message is of relaxed attentiveness—you have to be very relaxed and yet alert. And it is possible. And only this possibility will make you a whole man, a holy man. Otherwise you will remain half—

and a half man is always miserable. The West is miserable spiritually, the East is miserable materially. And man needs both.

With Buddha, a new age can dawn. And the secret is simple: learn relaxed awareness.

— Osho

THE MEDICINE OF
UNBORN UNDYING

"We come into this world alone,
We depart alone"--
This also is illusion.
I will teach you the way
Not to come, not to go!

We eat, excrete, sleep, and get up;
This is our world.
All we have to do after that
Is to die.

I shan't die, I shan't go anywhere,
I'll be here;
But don't ask me anything,
I shan't answer.

Whatsoever it may be,
It is all part of the world of illusion,
Death itself
Not being a real thing.

Should you wish to know the way
In both this world,
And that other,
Ask a man of mercy and sincerity.

A monk asks Master Pai-Chang,
"Who is the Buddha?"
Pai-Chang answers,
"Who are you?"

THE PURPOSE OF THE BUDDHAS IS NOT TO INFORM YOU but to transform you. They want to bring a radical change in your consciousness, they want to change your very roots. They want to bring new eyes to you, new clarity. Their purpose is not to inform. They are not there to transfer some knowledge but to transplant some being. They want to share their light with you--the purpose is not to inform but to enlighten.

Hence they don't bother what your question is. Their answers may sometimes look very irrelevant, absurd. They are not--but they have a totally different kind of relevancy. They are relevant to you, not to your question.

Now, this monk asks Master Pai-Chang, "Who is the Buddha?" And Pai-Chang answers, "Who are you?"

See the point: he is turning the whole question into a totally new dimension. He is not answering, in fact he is giving a deeper question than the monk had asked--he is answering with another question. "Who is the Buddha?"--the answer is easy, he could have said, "Gautam Siddhartha." But that is irrelevant; he is not interested in the history of thought, he is not interested in history at all. He is not concerned with a certain man called Gautam Buddha, he is more concerned with a certain awakening that can happen in everybody. That is real Buddhahood.

He turns the question towards the questioner himself. He makes a sword out of the question and pierces the very heart. He says: "Who are you? Don't ask me about Buddhas, just ask one question: 'Who am I?' and you will know who the Buddha is-- because everyone is carrying the potential of being a Buddha; there is no need to look outside yourself.

Lao Tzu says: To find truth, one need not go out of his room. One need not even open the door, one need not even open his eyes--because truth is your being. To know it is Buddhahood.

Remember it: the statements of Zen masters are not statements in the ordinary use of the word. They are not to convey something that you don't know. They are to shock you, provoke you, into a new quality of consciousness.

Listen to these sutras with this in your mind. Ikkyu is not propounding any philosophy. These are his shocks to his disciples--and they have immense beauty and immense potential to shock anybody. Listen:

"We come into this world alone,
We depart alone..."

This has been said again and again, down through the ages. All the religious people have been saying this: "We come alone into this world, we go alone." All togetherness is illusory. The very idea of togetherness arises because we are alone, and the aloneness hurts. We want to drown our aloneness in relationship....

That's why we become so much involved in love. Try to see the point. Ordinarily you think you have fallen in love with a woman or with a man because she is beautiful, he is beautiful. That is not the truth. The truth is just the opposite: you have fallen in love because you cannot be alone. And if a beautiful woman had not been available you would have fallen with an ugly woman too. So the beauty is not the question. If a woman had not been available at all you would have fallen with a man too. So the woman is not the question either.

You were going to fall. You were going to avoid yourself somehow or other. And there are people who don't fall in love with women or men--then they fall in love with money. They start moving into money or into a power trip, they become politicians That too is avoiding your aloneness. If you watch man, if you watch yourself deeply, you will be surprised--all your activities can be reduced to one single source. The source is that you are afraid of your aloneness. Everything else is just an excuse. The real cause is that you find yourself very alone.

And to be alone is to be miserable. There seems to be nowhere to go, no one to relate to, no one to drown oneself in. Poetry will do, music will do, sex will do, alcohol will do--but something is needed so you can drown your aloneness, so that you can forget that you are alone. This is the thorn in the soul that goes on hurting. And you go on changing your excuses.

The master's work is to bring you to the original cause. All your so-called love affairs are nothing but escapes. And I include all love affairs. The painter is in love with his paintings. And this is not an accident that if a man is too much involved in his poetry he will avoid women, because they will be a distraction. And women are naturally suspicious of a man who has any kind of hobby, any kind of interest, deep involvement, because then they feel jealous, then they know that he has another woman too. If a man is wed to science, the woman is as angry as if he were in love with some other woman. She does not want this science to stand between herself and him.

And the people who have been seekers and searchers and poets and painters, they have always remained bachelors. It is not just accidental. They have another kind of love affair; they don't need the woman, they don't need the man.

Just watch your mind. In one way and one thousand ways it is trying only one thing: "How to forget the fact that I am alone?"

Just the other day, I was reading these lines of T. S. Eliot:

Are we all in fact unloving and unlovable?
Then one is alone....

If love is not possible then one is alone. Love has to be made possible; if it is not possible it has to be created, believed in. If it is almost impossible then the illusion has to be created--because one needs to avoid one's aloneness.

When you are alone you are afraid. Remember, the fear does not come from ghosts. When you are alone the fear comes from your aloneness. But we go on hiding that cause, because to see that cause is to be transformed by seeing it. When you are moving in a forest alone you are not really afraid of ghosts or thieves or robbers, because they are more in the crowd. What would they be doing in the forest?--all their victims are available here.

When you are alone in the room and it is dark, you are not afraid of ghosts; ghosts are just projections. You are really afraid of your aloneness--that is the ghost. Suddenly you have to face yourself, suddenly you have to see your utter emptiness and aloneness and no way to relate. You have been shouting and shouting and nobody hears. You have been groping in the dark and you never come across a hand to hold you. You have been in this cold aloneness--nobody hugs you, nobody is there to hug you. Nobody is there to warm you.

This is the fear, the anguish of man. If love is not possible then one is alone. Hence love has to be made possible, it has to be created--even if it is pseudo, it has to be created. One has to go on loving, because otherwise it will be impossible to live.

And whenever a society comes across the fact that love is false, then two things become possible: either people start committing suicide, or people start becoming sannyasins. And both are the same. Suicide is an ordinary effort just to destroy yourself: if you are not there then nobody will be alone. But that doesn't work; you are soon in another body. That has never worked.

Sannyas is the ultimate suicide. If one is alone, then one is alone. It has to be accepted, it has not to be avoided: if one is alone, so what? If that is the fact, then that is the fact--then one has to go into it. Sannyas means encountering one's aloneness, going into it. Going into it in spite of all the fear. Dying into it. If death happens through it, it is okay, but one is not going to shirk from the truth. If aloneness is truth, then one accepts and goes into it. That's the meaning of sannyas. And one really commits suicide. One disappears.

This is the transformation I am talking about. Buddhas are not interested in information, they are interested in transformation. Your whole world is a great device to escape from yourself. Buddhas destroy your devices, they bring you back to yourself.

That's why it is only for the rare, the courageous, to be in contact with a Buddha. The ordinary mind cannot bear it; the presence of a Buddha is unbearable. Why? Why have people been so much against Buddha and Christ and Zarathustra and Lao Tzu? For a certain reason: these are the people who don't allow you the luxury of the untruth, the comfort of the lie, the convenience of living in illusions. These are the people who don't allow you; these are the people who go on forcing you towards the truth. And the truth is dangerous.

The first truth to experience is that one is alone. The first truth to experience is that love is illusory. Just think of it, just think of the enormity of it, that love is illusory. And you have lived only through that illusion...

You were in love with your parents, you were in love with your brothers and sisters, then you started falling in love with a woman or a man. You are in love with your country, your church, your religion, and you are in love with your car, and ice cream--and so on and so forth. You are living in all these illusions.

And suddenly you find yourself naked, alone, all illusions have disappeared. It hurts.

Just this morning, Vivek was saying--and she has been saying again and again with these Ikkyu discourses--"These discourses

are heavy, depressing." They are bound to be so, because
whenever any of your illusions are touched it creates great
restlessness. You become afraid; somehow you were managing it-
-and you know deep down that there is no bottom to it but you
don't want to look. Seeing will be frightening; you want to go on
remaining in the illusion.

Nobody wants to see that his love is false. People are ready to
believe that their past loves were false--but this? No, this love is
true. When it has disappeared they will say it was also false--but
then another love is true. In whatsoever illusion they are living,
they pretend that this one is true. "Others--Ikkyu may be right,
Osho may be right about other loves, they were false, we know.
But this one? This one is a totally different thing. This is not an
ordinary love, I have found my soul mate."

Nobody has ever found one--how can you find your soul mate?
Aloneness is absolute. These are just efforts to deceive yourself--
and you can go on deceiving. That's what you have been doing
down the ages, for so many lives...

But you forget. And you forget because of the birth trauma.
When the child is born he remembers--he remembers perfectly all
that has happened in the past life; he knows it. But the birth
trauma is such, the pain of being born is such... He lived in the
womb comfortably for nine months--never again will you be in such
comfort, not even an emperor can be in such comfort.

You were floating in warm liquid. And all needs were fulfilled,
and you had no responsibility, no worry. You were just fast asleep
and dreaming, dreaming sweet things. You were completely
protected, secure. Everything was happening of its own accord;
not a single effort was needed on your part.

And suddenly one day after nine months, all that world is
destroyed. You are uprooted. You were grounded in the womb,
you were connected with the mother: you are disconnected. And
you have to pass through the birth canal, which is a very narrow
canal.

The child feels immense pain. The pain is such that he becomes unconscious. That is a built-in mechanism in the mind-- whenever something becomes unbearable, the mind simply turns you off so that you need not feel it In fact, to call any pain unbearable is existentially wrong, because whenever pain becomes unbearable you become unconscious. So you have never known unbearable pain--if you know it, and you are conscious, it is still bearable. Once it reaches to the point where it becomes unbearable, immediately the whole mechanism for consciousness is turned off. You fall into a coma--a natural anesthesia.

So each child passing through the birth canal falls into a coma, and that disrupts his memory. And again he starts fooling around in the same old way, thinking that he is doing something new.

Nobody is doing anything new. All that you are doing you have done so many times, so many million times. It is nothing new. This anger, this greed, this sex, this ambition, this possessiveness--you have done it all millions of times. But because of the birth trauma there has been a discontinuity, a gap. And because of that gap your past is no more available to you.

Through deep primal scream the past can become available. If you can move backwards into the birth trauma you can remember your past lives. But you will have to move deep into the birth trauma. And once you have reached back into the womb-state of your consciousness, suddenly you will see your whole autobiography. And it is long. It is tedious--it is nothing but anguish, failure and frustration.

In the new commune, we are going to make efforts to make you remember your past lives. Then you will not think that these sayings of Ikkyu are depressive--then you will see these are the truths.

But you are living in an untrue life, thinking you are doing something new. And because you think it is new, you remain enchanted by it, by the magic of the new. If you can come to know that you have fallen in love millions of times, and each time it was a failure, it will be impossible to fall into the trap again, You will see that it is futile--that there is no soul mate, that there has never been. That aloneness is absolute. That there is no way to commune, there is no way to communicate. That nobody can understand you, and you cannot understand anybody.

I know these talks are bound to be depressive. Why? Because these talks will touch some wounds in you and the pus will start oozing out. And remember always: sometimes it is good to keep the wound open, because that is the condition for its cure. But courage is needed, certainly; without courage nothing can be done. To keep the wound open needs great courage--but that is the condition for its cure!

You would like to hide it. You would like to hide it behind flowers, you would like to forget about the wound. You would like to move into some consolation: "Maybe love has not happened yet--now it can happen. This time I may be able to make it."

But love cannot be possible. To make it possible is not a question that depends on you. Love itself is an impossibility. It keeps you deluded, it keeps you in a kind of dream state.

Ikkyu says:

"We come into this world alone,
We depart alone..."

Togetherness is illusory. Aloneness is more fundamental. Love is illusory, meditation is more fundamental--but ultimately that too is illusory. That's where Ikkyu goes one step ahead and takes the quantum leap. You have heard it said many times: "We come alone into this world, and we depart alone." But Ikkyu says:

This also is illusion.
I will teach you the way
Not to come, not to go!

That is Zen, pure Zen. The ordinary religion teaches: Love is illusory. Zen finally teaches: Even meditation is illusory. Let me make it clear to you. Love means togetherness--the possibility of being together, the possibility of being lost into each other, the possibility of communication, the possibility of relating. When love fails, utterly fails, you start moving towards meditation. Meditation means the capacity to be alone. They are polarities, love and meditation. Meditation means the capacity not to relate--there is no need to relate, one is enough unto oneself.

Many people go on clinging to the world of love; a few escape from it, and then they go on clinging to the world of meditation. Zen says: If you cling to the world of meditation, if you start clinging to your aloneness, you are still far away from the truth. Because if togetherness is false, how can aloneness be true?

This is the great revolution that Zen brings into the world of religion. If togetherness is false then aloneness can't be true either--because aloneness can be understood only in the context of togetherness. If love is false then meditation can't be true either. Those who have decided for meditation against love, they have chosen a polarity. And the polarity depends on the other.

Just think: if darkness is false, how can light be true? If pain is false, how can happiness be true? If birth is false, how can death be true? If 'I' is false, how can 'thou' be true?--or vice versa. They exist as pairs. Love and meditation are a couple, married for ever.

And if you observe silently the functioning of your mind, you will see it happening continuously....

You are in love with a person, and soon you start feeling you need your own space. That is the need for meditation--you may not look at it that way, but it is exactly that. Being together, you start feeling suffocated, crowded, crushed. And you start seeing the point that you need your own space. You would like to be alone for a few days.

Just the other day, I received a letter from a woman sannyasin. Her lover has left for the West and she was very much worried and tense, naturally, because she will be alone here without the lover. And he had to go for some reasons, for some responsibilities--he would have liked to stay with her, but he had to go. So she was very much troubled, in pain.

But she was surprised--when he left she felt like a burden had left her. She felt very good. She wrote a letter to me, feeling very guilty. Seems a kind of betrayal: your lover has gone and you are feeling happy! You should be crying, you should be weeping, you should be walking around with a long face so everybody knows that your lover is gone. And she is feeling so happy, as she has never felt in her life!

Now what is happening? No need to feel guilty. If people are aware, this will happen to everybody. Whenever your lover goes you will dance. So at last you can be alone! It can't be for long-- within a few days you will be tired of your aloneness and you will start hankering for the lover. This is a polarity.

Love creates the need to be alone--to be alone is bound to happen through love. And when you are alone, aloneness creates the need to love--it is bound to happen through being alone. They are partners, partners in the same business.

Zen says: People who have escaped to the Himalayas and are sitting in their caves alone are just as stupid as the people who are chasing women or chasing men and thinking that they are living their life. Both are stupid! because both have chosen the polarities.

And it is proved by thousands of years of experience that the man who sits in the cave in the Himalayas only thinks of the woman and nothing else. And of course he becomes more and more afraid of the woman--because she is coming even there, if not physically then psychologically. He becomes so fascinated that there are moments when he starts projecting the woman almost physically, as if she is there. He can start having hallucinations.

In the Indian scriptures there are stories of great rishis meditating in the Himalayas; then one day suddenly beautiful women from heaven come to distract them. Why should they be interested in distracting these poor people? for what?

Nobody comes, just hallucination. These people have lived too much in aloneness and are tired of aloneness, and now there is nobody to relate to. They create, they project. Their minds are in such need that they have to create somebody to talk to. And naturally, when you are going to create, why not create beautiful naked women dancing around you? That was their repression, that's why they had escaped from the world--it was there in them.

And have you seen the other point? A person sitting in the marketplace, tired, worried, tense, starts thinking how to renounce the world. He feels very good with even the idea: "One day I am going to renounce the world, and I will go to the Himalayas and be there with the Himalayan silence and the peace and the joy of it." Even the idea makes him feel good and fresh.

In India particularly, people go on thinking that one day or other they will renounce all this nonsense, this marketplace, and they will escape to a monastery and live there in happiness for ever. They can't--think about those women who come from heaven: they will come, they will torture you.

Meditation and love are part of one pair, one couple. They are together, they are married for ever--yin/yang, they cannot leave each other.

Hence Ikkyu is absolutely true when he says:

"We come into this world alone,
We depart alone"--
This also is illusion.

Love is illusion, so is meditation. The only thing that is good about meditation is that it can take you out of love. But don't cling to it--it is just a device to bring you out of your love. It brings you out of the illusion of love. But then immediately drop it too, otherwise you will start creating new illusions of meditation, kundalini arising, light happening in the chakras...and a thousand

and one things--'spiritual experiences' they are called. They are not spiritual or anything, they are just imagination.

You cannot live alone long. If the beautiful women are not coming, then kundalini will arise--something is going to happen, you cannot be alone. Maybe those beautiful women have forgotten or are too tired of the old rishis, and they don't come any more; or they are engaged on some other planets. Then something has to happen-- you will start seeing chakras moving inside you, energy arising. In your spine, a great rush; in your head, lotuses opening. You can't be alone! You are creating the world--now you call it spiritual.

What you call it doesn't matter. What matters is this simple phenomenon that you cannot be alone long. You cannot be together long, you cannot be alone long. Togetherness creates a need to be alone, to remain alone. And sooner or later you find that you are hankering for being together with somebody.

This is just day and night, summer and winter, it goes on moving--the wheel of life.

Ikkyu is right. He says: The truth is that one has to go beyond love and beyond meditation. One has to go beyond relatedness and one has to go beyond aloneness. When togetherness and aloneness have both disappeared, what is left? Nothing is left. That nothing is the taste of existence. You are neither alone nor together. In fact you are not.

I will teach you the way
Not to come, not to go!

And then where can you go? Then who is there to go? From where can you come? Who is there to come? Then all going and coming disappears, and that which always is, is known. The eternal is known. All coming and going is just dreams, time phenomena, soap bubbles, momentary.

When all those momentary things have been dropped, seeing that communication is not possible, relating is not possible, you start moving into aloneness. Then one day you see another phenomenon, that aloneness is not possible. Then rather than going back to love, which is the ordinary course, you jump out of aloneness too. You jump deeper.

From two you get into one, from one you get into none--no-one. That is *advaita*, that is the non-dual; you cannot even call it 'one'. And that is the source. That is the ocean, we are the waves of it. And seeing that ocean, you know you have never been born and you are not going to die either. Your whole existence was a dream existence. All has disappeared.

BUDDHA HAS CALLED this tendency to be in love or to be alone, the disposition of the ego to remain--either in relationship or in no relationship, but the ego wants to remain; either as a lover or as a meditator, either as a worldly man or as an other-worldly man, but the ego wants to remain--Buddha has called this disposition *avidya*, ignorance.

Remember, *avidya* does not mean non-knowledge. It simply means unawareness. *Avidya* is a disposition to treat the ego as an absolute. This creates a gap between man and the universe-- because of it, man is not in his right relation to the world. This falsification is called by Buddha *avidya*--ignorance, non-awareness.

You move into love in a kind of non-awareness, and you move into meditation also in a kind of non-awareness. If you become aware, love disappears, meditation disappears.

But let me remind you, otherwise you can misinterpret the whole thing: when what you call love disappears, another kind of love arises. You don't have any inkling of it. When meditation disappears then a totally different kind of meditativeness arises; you don't have any idea of it. Your meditation is effort--practice, cultivation, conditioning. When this meditation is dropped then a simple meditative quality arises in your being: you are simply silent, for no reason at all. Not that you are trying to be silent, not that you are trying to be still, not that you are making any efforts to remain tranquil. You are simply tranquil--because there is nobody to disturb. The ego is not there, the sole cause of disturbance is gone. You are simply quiet--not that you are trying to be quiet. Trying to be quiet simply means you are disturbed, split, divided in two parts--the one who is trying to make you silent, and the one who is being pulled and pummeled into silence. There is a kind of conflict--and how can conflict be meditative? There is enforcement, violence--and how can violence be peace?

That's why I say that those people who go on forcing yoga postures, mantras, upon themselves and somehow go on trying to maintain their peace are not peaceful people. They are just creating a facade, a hypocrisy.

When the true man arises in you, when the original man arises in you, there is no effort to be anything. One simply is. That is the natural man of Zen. He loves--not because he needs somebody, he loves because he can't help it. Love is there, love is flowing, and there is nobody to prevent it, so what can he do? He is meditative--not because he meditates, he is meditative because there is no disturbance found: the sole cause of disturbance, the ego, is no more there. The split is no more there, he is one. Collected, calm, integrated.

And all this is just spontaneous. That's why Zen people don't call the real man of Zen spiritual--he is neither worldly nor spiritual. He is in the world and yet not of it. He lives in the marketplace but the marketplace does not live in him.

Buddha's teaching is absolutely negative--for a certain reason. Love has to be negated, then meditation has to be negated. Now, these are the two highest things in the world, the most precious. And Buddha negates both.

Soren Kierkegaard, a Danish thinker and mystic, had a deep understanding about the negative teaching. He says that only negative teaching is possible, because any positive teaching, and the mind clings to it and creates new dreams about it. If you talk about God, mind clings to God--God becomes an object and mind starts thinking "How to relate to God? how to reach to God?" That becomes a love affair again. If you teach about *moksha*, paradise, then man starts becoming greedy about it: "How to grab it?" And the greed creates new dreams and new nightmares.

Only negative teaching is possible. A true teaching is bound to be negative, a true path is *via negativa*. Why? Because men are polemic against the truth, intentionally fleeing it. The purpose of negative teaching is to disturb and provoke man into being himself, since he is fleeing, negating himself. Negative teaching is negation of the negation.

Your whole life is negative; right now, negative. You are escaping from yourself--this is your negation. Now, this negation can be negated only by another negation. And when two negations meet, they cut each other, they destroy each other, they disappear into that fight.

And the positive is left. It cannot even be called positive--there is no negative left, so it cannot be called positive. It is the cosmic, the truth. The eternal, the ultimate, the absolute.

Buddha's path is of *neti neti*--neither this nor that. He says: Go on negating. A moment comes when nothing is found to negate any more, and that is the moment of nirvana. When nothing is left to negate, only nothingness in your hands, then freedom happens. You are freed from the self and all its projections.

We eat, excrete, sleep, and get up;
This is our world.
All we have to do after that
Is to die.

THIS STATEMENT HAS TWO MEANINGS. The first, for the ignorant man: this is your life, your whole life--see what your life consists of.

We eat, excrete, sleep, and get up;
This is our world.

That's what you have been doing. Mind must be utterly stupid,
otherwise just to do this--eating, excreting, sleeping, getting up
again...and the whole circle starts. This is your life. You move in
this way--day in, day out, year in, year out. Life in, life out, you go
on moving in this way.

All we have to do after that
Is to die.

Only one thing is left out of the circle, that is death. Sooner or
later, that too arrives. This is the whole story.

Omar Khayyam in his Rubaiyat says: "Some little talk a while of
me and thee there was, and then no more of thee and me." Just a
little talk, a repetitive talk, just a little gossiping. Eating, excreting,
sleeping and dying: this is all your life consists of.

But the question arises: But this is what even an enlightened
person goes on doing. What did Buddha do for forty years after he
became enlightened? What did Ikkyu himself do? For so many
years he remained enlightened on the earth; he was doing the
same.

Yes, but with a difference. That difference has to be
understood. Now, a Zen man lives as absolutely ordinarily as
everybody else, so you cannot make any other distinction. For
example, if you go and see a Jain monk he lives differently: he still
eats, excretes, sleeps, gets up, and the round moves on, but he
has made special ways of eating. He does not earn, he begs. For
excretion also he has made special ways; he excretes in an
extraordinary way. He does not go to the ordinary toilet, no--he has
to go outside the town. He cannot use your bathroom; he is no
ordinary human being.

Now, just see how foolishly we go on--extraordinary things. He goes outside the town. He eats only once a day. A certain sect of Jains is even more difficult: they eat standing. The Jain monk stands and eats, he remains naked, he never takes a bath, he never cleans his teeth. He does not sleep on a bed, just on the floor with straw under and over him. He has no shelter, he moves from one place to another, he is constantly on the move.

But these differences are in detail. Basically, whether you go outside the town to excrete, or you just use the ordinary toilet everybody is using, what is the difference? Whether you earn for yourself, or somebody else earns for you and you beg, what is the difference? Whether you eat twice, thrice or five times or once, does it make any difference? How does it make any difference? These are just habits, they can be cultivated.

There are tribes in Africa who eat only once in twenty-four hours. They have eaten that way for centuries, and they are accustomed to it. They cannot believe that people eat twice; once is enough.

Now, these differences in details are just to create the idea that "I am special." These are ego trips.

A Zen man simply lives as you live. It is very difficult to see the difference, but the difference is there. The difference is that he witnesses everything that is happening--that is the only difference. He eats, but he is a witness. Now, that is an interior difference. You cannot see it from the outside, but a little bit of it filters outside too. You can see a Zen man walking: he walks so consciously, so alertly. He eats consciously, alertly. He even sleeps consciously. A light remains burning even in his sleep, he goes on watching even his dreams. He is always on the watch--aware, conscious, alert. That is the difference.

And because he is alert, he remains relaxed. Because he is relaxed, the whole world is relaxed for him. It is the same world he lives in, but the roses are far more rosy and the green is far more green, and the call of the bird is an immense joy.

I have heard:

The patient was a beautiful young showgirl who complained of nervous tensions. The doctor prescribed a programme of tranquilizing pills and told her to come back in a couple of weeks and let him know how she felt.

When she returned, the doctor asked her if she felt any different and she replied: "No, doctor, but I've noticed that other people seem a lot more relaxed!"

If you are relaxed, you will suddenly see other people look a lot more relaxed. If you are silent, the whole world falls into a deep silence. If you are meditative, suddenly you become aware that trees are meditating, rocks are meditating. The moon is in deep meditation, so is the sun and the stars.

When love starts overflowing you--not the love that you know but the love that Buddhas know--when love starts flowing then you suddenly see it is flowing all over the place. It is flowing from the trees--you call it fragrance, it is love. It is radiating from the sun-- you call it light, it is love! It is the gravitation in the earth--you call it gravitation, it is love.

It is the silence of the night, the chirping of the birds, the flow in the river, the silence in the Himalayas.

When your love starts flowing, suddenly you become aware that love is flowing everywhere--that life consists of love, that existence is made of the stuff called love. But first it has to happen in you.

A man of Zen lives as ordinarily as you live. But his ordinariness is not ordinary. His ordinariness has an extra-ordinary quality in it: it radiates joy, celebration, it radiates witnessing.

A great Zen master, Lin Chi, says: "O Brethren in the Way, you must know that there is in the reality of Buddhism nothing extraordinary for you to perform. You just live as usual without even trying to do anything in particular, attending to your natural wants, putting on clothes, eating meals, and lying down if you feel tired. Let the ignorant people laugh at me. The wise men know what I mean to say."

Lin Chi is saying: Don't do anything in particular, don't be a doer. Let things happen, and be a watcher. And the ignorant will laugh at you; they will say, "What kind of religion is this?"

You must have come across these ignorant people. They will say to you, "What kind of religion is this? Into what trap have you fallen? Because your master is not teaching you anything special."

Yes, I am not teaching you anything special--because all ideas of speciality are ego trips. I am teaching you to be normal, to be ordinary. And if you can relax into normalcy, into ordinariness, suddenly you will burst forth into an extraordinary radiance. A great splendour will happen to you.

Lin Chi is right when he says, "Let the ignorant people laugh. The wise men know what I mean to say." Eat, drink and be merry, just as everybody else is. Don't try to be special in any way. But eating, remain a witness. Drinking, remain a witness. Merrying, remain a witness. And that witnessing will change everything. That witnessing is the transformation.

Only that witnessing will make you aware of who you are.

I shan't die, I shan't go anywhere,
I'll be here;
But don't ask me anything,
I shan't answer.

THIS IS IKKYU'S DEATH VERSE. Traditionally in Zen, when a master dies, his disciples ask him for a death verse--the last poetic expression, the last statement, the testament. The last statement about death.

Ikkyu says:

We eat, excrete, sleep, and get up;

This is our world.
All we have to do after that
Is to die.

Now death is coming, and the disciples have asked him to compose the last verse. And this was his last verse:

I shan't die, I shan't go anywhere,
I'll be here;
But don't ask me anything,
I shan't answer.

Somebody asked Raman Maharshi--he was dying, dying of cancer, and somebody asked, "When you are dead, where will you be gone?" And he opened his eyes and said, "Where can I go? I will be here." Because a man who is enlightened knows no other space than here, knows no other time than now. All time consists of now, and all space consists of here. Now-here is his whole existence.

Ikkyu says:

I shan't die...

Because in the first place I was never born. Birth is an illusion. And I am not going to die either--how can I die? because I was never born. Death is another illusion. I will be here, I have always been here. I am the taste of Tao. I am part of this eternity, I am a wave in this ocean. Sometimes as a wave, and sometimes as a no-wave--but I am here, and I am always here, and I will be always here. There is no coming, no going.

Ikkyu says:

I will teach you the way
Not to come, not to go!

Birth and death are both your ideas. It is very hard to understand that birth and death are both our ideas. When a man dies, in the last moments when he is dying he projects the birth idea. He starts thinking in the last moments: How to come back? in what form? His whole life's experiences become condensed into one form: a form arises.

He has lived in a certain way--he wanted to live in some other way, but could not make it. Now that other form takes possession of his mind: "Next time I would like to be this." And the last idea when one is dying becomes the seed.

If you can die without an idea, you will not be born. Your birth is your idea; it creates it. It is not just accidental that you are born; nothing is accidental. You have caused it, you are responsible for it. People die with different forms in their minds. Those forms become the guiding lines--then they enter into a womb according to those guiding lines. Birth arises.

And you will be surprised to know that death is also your idea. People die according to their ideas. In fact, depth psychology suspects that each death is a suicide. And the suspicion is almost true--I say 'almost' because I have to leave Buddhas out of it. But about everyone else it is true: your death is your idea.

You start becoming tired of life, sooner or later, and you start thinking how to die, how to disappear. It is too much. Enough is enough! Have you not thought many times of committing suicide?

Freud stumbled upon the idea; he called it 'thanatos'--the death-wish. Everybody has that, deep inside; it decides your death. Even people who die in accidents are people who are prone to accidents, who would like to die in an accident.

We go on creating possibilities around ourselves, and when they happen then we are surprised. Just watch your ideas and how they create your life. Somebody thinks that he is such a failure, he is never going to make anything. And he is not going to make anything, because this idea is creating his reality. And the more he finds that he is not making any way into anything, the more the idea becomes enforced by the feedback, and the more he will find he is becoming a failure. And a vicious circle is created.

The man who thinks he is going to succeed, he succeeds. The man who thinks he is going to be rich becomes rich, and the man who thinks he is not going to become rich remains poor. Try it. You will be surprised; sometimes you will not be able to believe it.

A man thinks he will never find anybody to be friendly with: he will not find--he has created a China Wall around himself, he is not available. He has to prove his idea right, remember. Even if somebody approaches with great friendliness, he will reject them. He has to prove his idea, he has a great commitment to his idea. He is not going to be distracted from his idea, his idea is so much a part of his ego. He has to show to the world that he was right, nobody can be a friend to him, that all are enemies. And all will turn, slowly slowly, into enemies.

Just watch your mind. You are constantly creating your life, you are constantly manufacturing your life.

Psychologists have come to the fact that people have had the idea, for centuries, that life consists of three score and ten years. That's why people live to nearabout seventy; there is no other reason. Because people believe that seventy years is the limit-- leave a few freaks who die a little earlier and a little later, but generally people follow the routine, the convention--they die at nearabout seventy. They start preparing, as they reach sixty they are getting ready. They get retirement, they start pulling themselves out of the world; they are getting ready. For ten years they will think, "Now it is coming. Three score and ten years. Now one year has passed: nine left. Two have passed: eight left." They are constantly hypnotizing themselves. And by seventy they are gone; they have proved their idea. And they have given the idea to their children also that this is how life is: only seventy years.

There are tribes which live longer. On the border of Kashmir in Pakistan, there is a tribe, Hunza--they live very long. One hundred is very easy, one hundred and twenty not difficult, one hundred and fifty also possible. But since they have come in contact with other people they have started dying earlier. Their food remains the same, everything remains the same--their climate, everything, is the same. But just because they have come to know that people die earlier, they must be feeling a little guilty. They have started dying earlier--one has to follow the crowd. Within thirty, forty years they will disappear. They will become part...three score and ten.

When Bernard Shaw was looking, in his old age...He lived long, when he was fifty he was looking for a place to live. He wanted to go out of London. And do you know how he found his place? A very psychological investigation he made. He went into cemeteries to look at the stones, what was written on them. He found one cemetery where people had lived very long--ninety, ninety-five, ninety-eight, one hundred...One man had died when he was a hundred, and on the stone there was an epitaph saying: "This man died untimely"--and he had lived a hundred years! He said, "This is the place to live." Where people think to die at a hundred is untimely, he chose that place to live. And he lived long--the idea worked.

Physiologists say that there seems to be no inner necessity in the physique of man to die. Yes, you will be surprised to know that there is a possibility one day that man can live very very long, almost a physical immortality--because the body goes on renewing itself. There is no need really for it to die, because it is constantly renewing itself. Old cells disappear, new cells arrive; within seven years the body changes itself completely. It continuously overhauls itself, renews, rejuvenates, it is a continuum. There is no inner necessity for the body to die.

Now physiologists agree about it. And psychologists also are feeling that the reason why people die may be something to do with the mind, not with the body.

This is one of the greatest teachings of Buddhism--that birth is mind, death is mind. All ideas. And you are neither.

I shan't die, I shan't go anywhere,
I'll be here;
But don't ask me anything,
I shan't answer.

Because it can't be answered. It has to be lived, seen. It has to be tasted. Just go deep inside yourself, watch: are you thinking to die? Then you are creating the seed. In fact, birth creates death.

Just a few moments before, I told you about the birth trauma. When a child is born the child thinks this is a death. Naturally, because he was living so beautifully. He is being thrown out of paradise. Adam is expelled in every child--he was in the Garden of Eden, now he is being expelled. That was life, and this seems to be death.

And each child, the whole of his life, wants to get back into the womb of the mother. We create substitute wombs. Our bedrooms are wombs--the closed bedroom with dark curtains, in the night you put the light off, it is dark, as dark as it is in the womb. Then the bed, the cozy bed, the pillows, the mattress, the blankets--and you snuggle into the blanket, and you take the womb posture. The warmth of the bed, the darkness all around, the comfort, the silence...you are again slipping back into the womb.

Each sleep every night is a re-enactment of the womb; it is a small death. That's why you find it so hard to get up in the morning--because getting up in the morning again disturbs your deep unconscious. It is again a birth--the birth trauma is still affecting you.

You will be surprised that primitive people don't have any trouble getting up early in the morning. By the time the sun rises they are up, no problem at all. And the reason is because they don't have that much birth trauma. In a primitive society the child is not born with such suffering as happens with civilized people. The mother does not go through great pain. It is very simple, it is just like animals.

The mother may be working in the field and she will give birth to the child and carry the child home. Or maybe it was mid-noon and the work was not complete--she will keep the child by the side of the tree, she will finish the work and then take the child back home. No hospitalization is needed, no drugs are needed, she feels no pain. On the contrary, she feels great ecstasy. More orgasmic is the experience of giving birth to a child than any sexual experience can ever be. And the child comes so easily that he has no birth trauma.

That's why in primitive societies people get up early in the morning. The more a society becomes civilized, the more it becomes difficult...

The other day I inquired about Padma, and she was asleep at eleven o'clock. Must have suffered a great birth trauma. If you have suffered a great birth trauma then every morning you feel it very difficult to get up; your whole body wants to remain in the bed. That is, your body wants to remain in the womb--it does not want to get out of it, you have to be pulled out of it.

Birth creates death. Each sleep is a small death. That's why many people find it very difficult to make love in bed, because it stirs the idea of death. They become a little afraid. They find it far better to make love in a car or on the beach, but to make love in bed feels a little difficult. For a few people it is really impossible, because the whole idea of the bed conjures up the atmosphere of death.

But for a few other people it is only possible to make love in bed--because entering into the body of a woman they think of entering into the womb again. It depends what your thinking is. If you think that entering the body of a woman is entering into the womb again, then you will not find any other place to make love except the bed. But if you feel afraid of death and if the birth trauma stirs memories in you, then it will be difficult to be orgasmic in bed.

People die in their beds. Ninety-nine percent of people die in their beds. Naturally--that seems to be the natural thing: one day they disappear in bed. And for the whole life they think how to create the womb again. Your houses are a recreation of the womb. The more close a thing comes to the womb, the more comfortable it feels.

I shan't die, I shan't go anywhere,
I'll be here;
But don't ask me anything,
I shan't answer.

Death is false, as false as birth. You are beyond birth and beyond death. You come into birth, you take the form of the birth, and then you move beyond that form in death--but you are formless. But nothing can be said about it. It has to be experienced.

Whatsoever it may be,
It is all part of the world of illusion,
Death itself
Not being a real thing.

Death is the greatest illusion, next only to birth. You are eternal.

Ikkyu used to call his approach towards birth and death "the medicine of unborn undying". He used to say, "This can cure all ills"--because all ills are somewhere in between birth and death. If you can drop the idea of birth and death, then everything is dropped. Then you need not be worried about love and you need not be worried about meditation. Then there is no togetherness and no aloneness.

You are one with the whole. How can you be alone? And how can you be together?--because there is nobody other than the whole. The whole is the whole--nothing besides, nothing outside it--so it cannot be together with anybody. That's why togetherness is impossible. But you cannot be alone either, because the very idea "I am alone" makes you feel separate from the whole. You are in it. You are it.

Should you wish to know the way
In both this world,
And that other,
Ask a man of mercy and sincerity.

IKKYU SAYS: Don't ask me, I will not answer. First, the experience is such, it can't be answered. But one thing can be done, that's what Buddhas go on doing: they point the way. They don't say what will happen, what happens, but they say how it can happen.

Should you wish to know the way...

Never ask about the experience, it is inexpressible. But ask about the way, then something can be said--how to move into it, what devices to use, from where to start, how to get out of the vicious circle. How to move out of love: meditation will help. How to get out of meditation: trusting life will help.

And when you are out of meditation and out of love, love will happen and meditation will happen of their own accord. Then they will not be tiny things created by you, they will be gifts of God.

Should you wish to know the way
In both this world,
And that other,
Ask a man of mercy and sincerity.

But how to find a Buddha? Two things, Ikkyu says: sincerity and mercy. His compassion will give you the idea--his love, his overflowing love, for no reason at all.

If you can find a man of love...remember those words: "One glimpse of the real man, and you are in love." Then you are love. If you can find a man of love then don't miss the opportunity. He is the door: enter into him. And you will find sincerity.

Remember, sincerity does not mean seriousness. It means truthfulness, it means authenticity. And how will you judge whether the man is authentic, truthful, or not? There is only one thing to remember: truth is paradoxical. Only untruth is consistent. If you find a man very consistent, avoid him, because that means he is simply philosophizing. He has not yet experienced anything, he is not a sincere man.

A sincere man is one who simply says whatsoever is the case-- whether it contradicts him, whether it is consistent or inconsistent, makes no difference to him.

Remember the Zen definition of truth: A truth is that whose contradictory is also true. So a man of sincerity is bound to be paradoxical. And that is where we miss. If you come across paradoxes you think, "This is an inconsistent man; how can he be true?" You have an idea that truth has to be consistent--and that prevents you from finding Buddhas. And you fall in the trap of logicians, philosophers, thinkers.

A Buddha is basically, fundamentally, tacitly, paradox--because he sees the truth in its totality. And the totality is paradoxical. The totality is both: night and day, love and meditation. The totality is both: this and that, visible, invisible. The totality is both birth and death, and neither. The totality means the whole thing is so complex, you cannot make any consistent statement about it. You have to go on contradicting yourself.

If you can find a man of contradictions, you may be close to somebody who knows. Truth is that whose contradictory is also true.

Look for the sincerity through the paradox. He is so sincere that he is ready to become inconsistent. His sincerity is such that he is ready to be called mad. His sincerity is such that he does not try to convince you through logic. He is not a salesman. He is not worried about convincing you. He simply states whatsoever is the case--whether you are convinced or not convinced, that is up to you. He is not in any way interested in forcing something upon you. He is ready to help, but not to coerce you.

And what is mercy? It does not mean pity. Buddhas don't pity you, because pity arises out of ego. They are merciful, they are compassionate--and the difference is great.

Just the other day, somebody asked me a question: "The groups, therapy groups, that are run here are very hard, cruel. How do you allow them, a man of compassion?" And not only that, he mentions the incident that I mentioned some days before, that one of my friends was going to commit suicide. He mentions that "Listening to that story, I thought you are also very cruel. You didn't persuade the man not to commit suicide; on the contrary, you were ready to take him to the river to jump from the cliff and die. What kind of compassion is this?"

You missed the whole story. He was saved! You missed that point. It is not how he was saved--the point is that he was saved. Look at the result.

A compassionate man looks at the result. What devices he uses are not important. He is ready to use any device--just look at the objective result. A compassionate man is not sentimental, emotional. You would have liked me to hug him and cry...But then he would have committed suicide! Would it have been compassion? I would have driven him to suicide. That's what his parents, his mother and father and friends, were doing, they were driving him to commit suicide. The more they were trying to persuade him, the more he was trying to say no. In fact he was getting more and more excited about suicide, because of these people, because of their attention. And they were all loving people, they loved the man--but see the difference.

These are the two kinds of love. One is sentimental and emotional; it doesn't help. Another is objective love; it helps. But then the person who is full of objective love decides how to move. His sole concern is how to save people.

I wanted to save this friend, that's why I was so cruel. And I want you also to be saved, that's why all the therapy groups here are cruel. Sometimes even people who should be more knowing, misunderstand.

That's what happened to one of the sannyasins, Geet Govind. He had come from Esalen, he is a co-founder of Esalen, so he knows everything about therapy groups. But he does not know anything about me. He does not know anything about objective compassion. Seeing the encounter group here, he was very much shaken. And he was not even courageous enough to say it to me-- because after the encounter group I had especially asked him, "What do you think, Geet Govind?" And he said, "All is good, everything is good, I enjoyed it"--or things like that.

But back home, he started spreading the news around, "Don't go to Poona. Those people are dangerous, the groups are very violent and cruel."

He misunderstood the whole point. But that's what happens to knowledgeable people. Because he thinks he knows--and he knows about encounter groups, but he does not know that when an encounter group is used by a compassionate man it is a totally different thing. He knows about therapy, but he does not know anything about Buddhas.

Here, the therapy groups are not just therapy groups as they are in Esalen. Here they are used just as devices--to destroy something, to shake you into awakening. The whole point is to shake you out of your sleep. And all kinds of things will be used. If sometimes a dagger needs to be put into your heart, it has to be used. If a sword is needed then it has to be used.

Do you remember Jesus' saying? "I have come into the world not to bring peace but to bring a sword." What does he mean? A man of compassion! Only something like a sword can shake you out of your sleep.

So when you come across a man of mercy, remember: his whole point is how to awaken you. He is not sentimental, he will not cry with you; he will be very objective and very scientific. But he feels for you, he loves you, he wants to help you. And only he can help you. All those sentimental people and all that sentimental nonsense is not going to help. If it was going to help, you would have already been saved.

So whenever you can find a man of sincerity, a man of paradox, truth, whose whole concern is truth...Even if it makes him seem contradictory he is ready; he does not change the truth just to become consistent. And his whole concern is to help people become alert and aware--even if sometimes cruel methods are needed he is ready to use them. That is the man of compassion and sincerity.

And only a man of compassion and sincerity can be a master. Avoid those who console you. Follow those who are ready to destroy you--because only when you are destroyed, God is born.

IT AIN'T EASY!

What is the desire for perfection?

I'm feeling unspiritual and stupid,
like an orange vegetable.
Am I going off the track?

I know of only two stages:
the master and the disciple.
Is there a third stage--
self-sufficient fully grown-up person?

How can you make generalizations
about men and women?
You've made me angry!

The first question

What is the desire for perfection?

ADHEERA, THE DESIRE FOR PERFECTION is the search for the lost womb. The paradise--lost. The child is utterly happy in the mother's womb; that memory persists. It is not just a memory in the brain, it is in every cell of the body, every fiber of the body. It is all over you.

That memory persists. Those nine months have been of such eternal joy, of such relaxation and let-go, it is not easy to forget it. Even though consciously you have forgotten about it--because of the birth trauma you became disconnected consciously from it--yet the unconscious still hankers for it. It tries in every way to reach to that lost paradise again.

The whole of religion consists of that search, and the whole of science too consists of that search. The scientific endeavour is to create that womb outside--with central heating, with central air-conditioning, with better clothes, with better technology--the whole effort is to create the womb outside.

And religion tries to create the womb inside--with prayer, with meditation techniques, with love, with God. But the effort is one: how to be again in those beautiful days. That lost womb is the source of the parable of Adam, Eve and the Garden of Eden.

You ask: What is the desire for perfection?

The desire for perfection is that whatsoever is the case with you, it is never up to the mark. It is never as it should be, there is a gap. You can still imagine things being better; you can still imagine better days, better possibilities. One goes on hankering for those better possibilities.

You can drop this search for perfection only if you move back through the birth trauma again. If you live it consciously and you remember consciously those days in the womb, immediately the desire for perfection will disappear; it disappears immediately. And the disappearance of this desire is a great relief, because only then can you start living moment-to-moment--how can you live with this desire for perfection? It is the source of all neurosis.

The man who wants to become perfect is bound to become neurotic, because he can't be here. He is in the future, which is not. He cannot enjoy this moment, he can only condemn it. He cannot love this woman because he has the idea of a perfect woman. He cannot love this man because this man is not perfect. He cannot enjoy this food, this breakfast, this morning--nothing is ever fulfilling to him, can't be. His expectation is there and he is continuously comparing, and continuously falling short.

The man who lives in the desire for perfection, lives a condemned life. And the society helps it too. The parents, the schools, the colleges, the universities, the mahatmas, the priests, the politicians, they all help to make you neurotic.

From the very childhood, you have not been accepted as you are. You have been told, "Be like this, only then are you acceptable." If you want to live a life of your own you will be condemned by everybody, everybody will be against you. Your parents will not be able to tolerate you. They have to mould you, form you, change you, manipulate you--they have to manufacture you according to their hearts' desire.

And what is the problem with them? They are also suffering

from the birth trauma. They have tried their whole life to become perfect, and they have failed. Nobody can ever succeed; the desire is such that it is bound to fail. Failure is inevitable--because you can go on succeeding, but with you the idea of perfection starts becoming more and more sophisticated. As you succeed, the idea starts receding further ahead into the future. It becomes more sophisticated: more expectations...

The distance between you and the idea of perfection remains the same. If you have ten thousand rupees, you need one hundred thousand to be happy. When you have one hundred thousand, the desire has moved ahead; now that is not enough. And so is the case in everything.

The parents are living their own traumas. They have tried their whole life and they have failed; now they want to live through the child. Hence they start turning the child into a neurotic being, now they start teaching the child. This is a vicarious way of living. They have failed; now they know that death is coming, now their days are finished, now they are losing hope. A new hope arises, they can live through the child. If they were not perfect, at least their children can be perfect. And they say a tree is known by the fruit: if the children are perfect then the parents must have been perfect.

This is how the whole neurosis continues, from one generation to another generation. The parents are continuously trying to improve upon the child in every way. And all that they succeed in doing is, they make the child feel condemned as he is. They make it impossible for the child to love himself, to respect himself. And once that love and respect for oneself is lost, one is lost.

The world suffers so much--from madness, all kinds of mental illnesses, physical diseases. And ninety-nine percent of the causes of all these mind-body problems come from this approach, that the child has to be perfect.

A family was seated in a restaurant. The waitress took the order of the adults and then turned to their young son.

"What will you have, sonny?" she asked.

"I want a hot dog," the boy began timidly.

Before the waitress could write down the order, the mother interrupted. "No, no hot dog," she said. "Give him potatoes, beef, and some carrots."

But the waitress ignored her completely. "Do you want some ketchup or mustard on your hot dog?" she asked of the boy.

"Ketchup," he replied with a happy smile on his face.

"Coming up," the waitress said, starting for the kitchen.

There was stunned silence upon her departure. Finally, the boy turned to his parents. "Know what?" he said. "She thinks I'm real."

That is from where the problem is arising, you don't allow your children to be real. You make them feel unreal, you force them to feel phony, rejected, worthless. And once this idea is created in their minds, that they are worthless as they are, naturally a great desire to become perfect arises. And with that arise all sorts of neuroses.

My effort here is to help you, not to be perfect, but to drop the whole nonsense. In dropping that, you will become for the first time real.

Reality is never perfect, remember. Reality is always growing-- how can it be perfect? Once something is perfect, growth is not possible. Only imperfection can have the joy of growing.

Do you want to remain a flower, growing, opening? Or do you want to become just a dead stone--perfect, no opening, no growing, no change? Remain imperfect and respect your imperfections, and you will be able to enjoy, celebrate, and you will be able to be healthy and whole. And you will not need to go to a psychiatrist or a psychoanalyst and lie down stupidly on the couch for five years talking nonsense. And there will be no need for any shock treatments either. In fact, if your mental stress disappears, your body will feel immediately relieved.

Many diseases will automatically disappear from the earth if this foolish idea to become perfect disappears. But this has been taught from every nook and corner--from the church, from the temple, from the mosque, from the university. Everywhere, everyone seems to be part of the conspiracy. Everyone seems to be utterly determined to make every person perfect. And not even a single perfect human being has ever existed--cannot exist. Imperfection is the way things are. Imperfection is beautiful, because it has the potential to grow and flow. Perfection is simply death and nothing else.

Life is imperfect. And life enjoys imperfection.

I teach you totality, not perfection. And these are two different goals. Perfection is a neurotic goal, totality is a sane goal. Perfection is in the future, totality is herenow. You can be total this moment. You can be total in your anger, you can be total in your sex, you can be total in whatsoever you are doing--cleaning the floor or cooking food or writing poetry. You can be total! This moment! It needs no preparation, it needs no cultivation.

And by being total you will enter into God, into nirvana. When you are total, the self disappears--that is the beauty of totality. Just try to understand--this is subtle, and of immense significance: when you are total, the self disappears.

Have you ever seen any total moments? Then you know, the self immediately disappears. If you are totally in love with a woman or a man, the self disappears. When you are making love the self disappears, if you are total in it. If you have gone for a morning walk and you are total in it, nothing else matters in those beautiful moments--just the morning and you, you and the morning, the birds and the trees and the sun, and you are completely drowned, utterly drowned in the moment--the self disappears.

The disappearance of the self is benediction. You will know what Buddha means by 'no-self'. He means utter bliss. He never uses the words 'utter bliss' because he knows you--you can make a goal out of it, you can start striving to utter bliss. You can make a goal of the perfectionist--you can say, "I cannot rest unless I become perfectly blissful." Now you have missed the whole point.

If you are total, bliss happens as a by-product, because self disappears. Dancing, singing, listening to music--or just here, being with me, sometimes it happens. I can see it happening to many people. I know when I look at your face whether there is self or not. Your face immediately has a different quality. When I look at you and the self is not there, you are just an opening, a window, I can see God clearly in you. In those moments, God is there, you are not. All clouds have disappeared and the sky is clear, transparent, and the sun is shining.

Whenever your self disappears for a moment, suddenly I can see the luminousness that comes to your face, that quality of magic that arises around you.

But we have been taught to live in a non-total way, through the idea of perfection.

I teach you totality. In totality, self disappears. And just the contrary is the case with perfection. With the idea of perfection the self is strengthened. It is an egoist ideal: "I want to be perfect." 'I' cannot be total, because in totality no 'I' is ever found. Hence it appeals to the ego too, to become perfect, to be the most perfect man or woman in the world. The ego feels very good, the ego starts striving for it. The ego is involved with the idea of perfection.

With the experience of totality, the ego is simply non-existential. If you learn how to be herenow, slowly slowly you will see that life is beautiful as it is. Life is beautiful in its suchness, in its *as-it-is-ness*. It needs no improvement.

This can be helped through the birth trauma--if you go through the birth trauma, if you live it consciously again, then the whole significance of birth changes.

Right now the womb experience remains in your unconscious-- so important that you are striving for it unknowingly. That's why people go on thinking that in the past, everything was good. This is nothing but a projection because of the womb experience. In all the societies of the world, in all the religions of the world, the idea persists that the golden age was there somewhere in the past.

When Adam lived in the Garden of Eden, it was paradise. In India, they say the golden age was very very prehistoric. Then things started falling down--the original sin. We were in a state of bliss and then we started falling. Then we lost it.

This is nothing but the same story, woven philosophically. The original fall is nothing but the fall from the womb. And the memory that before, some time before, far away in the past, everything was golden and beautiful, is nothing but a memory projected on history. Individual memory projected on collective history. And we have to attain to it again, so we become interested in the future.

The past is important, the future is important, only the present is not important. Because we have lost the past--and only in the future, trying, striving, reaching it, some day we will find it.

So there are two types of people, and both are not different basically. Religious people say the golden age was in the past. And the non-religious say the golden age is going to be in the future, the utopia is coming. Hindus say the golden age--*satyayuga*, the age of truth--was in the past. And communists say the age, the golden age--*Samyuga*, the age of equality--is going to come in the future.

They are not different. They look different, because one talks about the past, another talks about the future. But the mechanism is the same: they both want to avoid the present. Communists and anti-communists are not very different.

Real spirituality begins with the present and ends with the present. It has no past, it has no future. This moment is all.

So, Adheera, try to get consciously into your unconscious. Try to penetrate to where this desire for perfection is arising. Go into your childhood. You have been taught, you have been conditioned layer upon layer, you will have to peel your onion of the mind. And then finally you will come to the birth trauma, the day you were born.

You can live it again. That is the whole process of rebirthing: you can live it again. And once you live it again, it disappears. And what happens? The total perspective changes. If you can live it again consciously--if you can move back, become a child, a small child, a baby, just coming out of the womb--you will go through a great suffering and agony. You will suffer the same birth pain; you will feel suffocated, your breathing will become hectic. Sometimes the breathing may stop completely, your body will become paralyzed. You may feel you are dying, because that's what you felt when you were coming out of the womb.

You will feel you are passing through a very narrow tunnel, suffocating, dark. Great fear will arise in your being, you will be shaken and rocked by the fear. You will need somebody to help you.

Hence the need for a master. You will need somebody to protect you, you will need somebody to support you--to tell you, "Don't be afraid, go into it. Let it pass, don't escape from it." Once you have passed through it and once you have seen consciously what happened in your birth unconsciously, it is wiped out. This is the process of the mind. Anything lived consciously is wiped out; it has no more grip on your unconscious being.

And then for the first time you open your eyes and you see that the world is beautiful. The willow is green and the rose is red. And then for the first time you see that the womb was good but it is not the goal. The womb was convenient but it was only a preparation. It was not real life; it was a sucker's life, it was pure exploitation. It was dependence. It knew nothing of freedom--how can it be beautiful? Yes, it was convenient and comfortable, but you were simply vegetating, you were not really alive. You were a contented pig. It has no worth in itself.

And then you start seeing that life has beauties which no womb can ever give to you.

All wombs are confined. That's why after nine months a child has to come out of it, because of the confinement. All wombs are prisons--comfortable, warm, but a prison is a prison. Even if it is comfortable, even if it is warm, it does not make it anything else; it is prison.

You are coming out of the womb into freedom. The whole sky opens up, and the sun and the moon and the trees and the stars-- they were not available to you. And the songs of the birds and the music and all the poetry and love--they were not available to you. Your paradise was not much of a paradise, your paradise was just a very stupid paradise.

Once you have seen that it was nothing of worth.... It was needed in those moments because you were growing and you were very tender and delicate and you needed the protection. Once the child is nine months he hankers to come out, he wants to come out, he wants to be free of the womb. He is ready to go into the world and see the joys and the miseries of the world. He is ready to go deep into experiences and into existence.

Once you have lived the birth trauma consciously and you have erased the pain memory, you will be surprised that something like a mist from your eyes has disappeared. And when you open your eyes the trees will be greener than they had ever been, and everything will be totally different. You will see the world in psychedelic colours--you will not need any drug trip for it.

People are taking drugs just to create something which is very natural. There is no need to destroy your body chemically for it. You can just go through the birth trauma, and you can come back, and the whole world and the whole experience of the world becomes psychedelic.

It is more colourful. It is a constant jubilation. There is no end to this jubilation--from beginningless beginning to endless end, it continues. It is a song ad infinitum.

Once you start seeing this, life begins. That's what Jesus means when he says, "Unless you are born again, you will not enter into my kingdom of God." He is talking about rebirthing!

In the East, we have a name for a man who has become alert and total, we call him *dwija*--twice-born. He has attained to a second birth. The first birth is bound to be unconscious. And if you live only with the first birth, you will remain a perfectionist. Once you are twice-born, consciously born, and have erased all the pain-memory of the first birth, you will live the life of totality. Not with the desire for perfection--all desire for perfection disappears, because you see this is the most perfect world, and you are the most perfect person, and everybody is perfect, and all is as it should be.

When you see all is as it should be, great gratitude arises. Prayer is natural. You bow down to the earth, you bow down to the sun, you bow down to existence. That is the religious quality--not that you go to church and think you are religious, and you bow down to Christ and think you are religious: you are not! Nothing of the sort. You are simply afraid; you are thinking Christ will save you.

Nobody can save you, unless you save yourself. No Christ, no Buddha, can save you. But you can save yourself. And it is your responsibility to save yourself. And the way to save yourself is to be reborn, born again.

Remember, if you suffer from the desire for perfection--and almost everybody does--then make it a point that you have to go back into your birth process and you have to erase the whole tape. And then look again with empty eyes, and you will be surprised.

I have been working on many people. And whenever they come across their birth memory, strange unbelievable things happen. I was helping a young man to go through. He came to a point when he almost started suffocating--crying, weeping, and then he became paralyzed. For a moment, everything stopped--even breathing. It was such agony. Then he opened his eyes, looked at me, and he said, "This is strange. I am smelling chloroform and the smell that surrounds a hospital."

I asked him, "Were you born in a hospital?" He said, "I don't know, I have never asked my mother." We checked with the mother and she said, "Yes, he was born in a hospital. And I was in such pain that I was given a heavy dose of chloroform."

The memory of the chloroform entered into his cells. He could still smell it--after twenty-eight years!

But once you pass through all these memories they start losing their control over you. Going through the birth is the first step. If you can do it, then the second step is going through the death that preceded your birth, nine months before. If you can go through your birth, you can easily go through your death. And once you have gone through your death, your past life becomes available to you. And then the whole stupidity of it....

That's why these Buddha sayings, these Ikkyu sutras, look so depressing to you--because they are based on a totally different understanding of life. These people have known their past lives and they see the stupidity of it. You cannot see. You think you are doing great things; you are not aware.

If you have been in love for many many lives, again and again, and always failed and failed and failed, and if you come to know about it, if you can see it, then the love affair that you are in today will simply become invalid, just through that experience. Now you know that these are the ways you have always been deceiving yourself. And it is a repetition, a wheel that goes on moving.

These sutras are not philosophical sutras, they don't propound a doctrine. They are based on a totally different experience of life, on a different vision. So sometimes you will feel disturbed.

The other day, Arup was saying to somebody, "These heavy talks, and Osho has called the series 'Take It Easy'!"

That's why I have called it 'Take It Easy'. It ain't easy. It is difficult to take it, it is very difficult to take it. It is almost impossible to take it, because it will shatter your whole life pattern. It ain't easy, that's why I have called the whole series 'Take It Easy'.

Truth is that whose contradictory is also true.

The second question

Since I have been here this time I have been feeling increasingly unspiritual and more and more stupid--like an orange vegetable. I feel to be enjoying sensual pleasures and in general to be very hedonistic. This doesn't fit with my previous feelings and ideas about being close to a master. What is happening? Am I going off the track?

What to do?

NISEEMA, THE REAL MASTER NEVER FITS WITH YOUR EXPECTATIONS. And if he fits he is not a master. The real master cannot fit with your expectations, your expectations come out of your mind. Your mind is the problem: it has to go down the drain, in toto.

A real master never fits with your expectations. And those who fit with your expectations are just businessmen, not real masters. They fit, they have to fit--that's how they depend on you. A real master is always a shock, a shattering. He will not in any way allow himself to fit with you. Then only can he destroy you.

A real master is not a consolation. A real master has to uncreate you--how can he be a consolation? He has to demolish you; he is not a renovation. He is not just patching up things, he has to uproot you from the very roots and transform you to another dimension. He is a transmutation. Nothing will ever fit with a real master.

Do you think Jews were unnecessarily angry with Jesus? The anger was this, that he didn't fit with their expectation.

He used to move with people who were not respectable. He used to live with people who were gamblers, drunkards, thieves. He used to stay in houses where no respectable person, no rabbi, would be ready to go. He allowed this prostitute, Magdalene, to become his closest disciple. He was not fitting with their expectations. A religious person should behave in a certain way-- he was behaving outrageously, he was annoying people.

Now, you ask me: Since I have been here this I have been feeling increasingly unspiritual.

That is your truth. And I am here to bring your truth to the surface. You must have been repressing what you call 'unspiritual'. In calling it unspiritual you simply say that you are against it; you are condemning it. Our words are significant. When you call something unspiritual you have condemned it.

You say: Since I have been here this time I have been feeling increasingly unspiritual.

You are becoming increasingly real, that's all. All your ideas of spirituality are being taken away. They were forced, pseudo. You were just repressing your reality and calling it spirituality. You were against yourself: You were not enjoying your being; you were crippling it, poisoning it. You were a victim. Now you are gathering courage to be yourself. Don't call it unspiritual; you are becoming real, you are becoming natural.

And how can nature be unspiritual and how can reality be unspiritual?

To be with me means first I have to take all that is pseudo in you. The false has to be known as false. And knowing it as false, it drops. The true can arrive only when the false has disappeared.

Now, your spirituality was false, Niseema. It was just a facade, it was a show-window spirituality. Deep down, you were always that which you are finding yourself now. Now your depth is meeting with your surface; they are losing the division, the split. You are relaxing, you are dropping the conflict with yourself. The top dog and the bottom dog are meeting, for the first time there is a merger happening. This is the beginning of growth, because only the real can grow. The plastic, the synthetic, the false, cannot grow.

You can have plastic flowers, but they cannot grow. Growth happens only to the real and your spirituality was like a plastic flower. That's how people are spiritual. Deep down they are absolutely the opposite, on the surface they have painted faces.

I am taking your painted face away, I am taking your mask away, the mask is slipping off. Hence this question has arisen. You must be becoming afraid: "What kind of master is this? And what am I doing here?" You must have come here expecting that you would become more spiritual, and I am making you more real! In your words, more 'unspiritual'.

Since I have been here this time I have been feeling increasingly unspiritual and more and more stupid.

That is a good beginning. To feel that one is ignorant is the beginning of wisdom. Only stupid people never feel that they are stupid. This is how wisdom arises--when you start seeing the stupidity of it all, something has happened in you, a ray of light has entered.

To move into the world of understanding, first one has to drop all kinds of knowledge. So I am taking your pseudo-spirituality and I am also taking your borrowed knowledge. The so-called spiritual people carry great knowledge--esoteric, occult, they go on collecting it. They consult I Ching and they consult astrology books and they read tarot cards and they go into the mysteries of *kabala*. And all are just mind games. They have nothing to do with spirituality, they are really meant for stupid people to play around with. And these people go on reading the Bible and the Vedas and the Gita--and they cram it, they become parrots. And the they think they know.

Knowledge is not knowing. Anything borrowed can never be your knowing.

So when you come to me, many things are going to happen. Each day you will feel poorer and poorer, and you had come to become richer and richer. So naturally, only the very courageous can stay with me, otherwise people escape. Because who wants to become poorer? You had come with so much knowledge and now you feel stupid. Now what kind of game is this? You had come to learn something, but what I am proposing here is not learning but unlearning.

You had come to accumulate a little bit more. You had already a beautiful collection of knowledge, you wanted to make it more up-to-date. You wanted to have something from a modern Buddha. Because the old Buddha is twenty-five centuries old, and things have changed. You wanted an up-to-date version of Buddhahood. And you come here and I start taking things away from you. Your knowledge starts disappearing and you feel in a panic: what is happening? You start feeling stupid.

You have always been stupid! Just that knowledge was giving you the idea that you are not. Now this is a great revelation. Your spirituality starts looking false, plastic--and you have been thinking that you are a saint, almost on the verge of enlightenment. And all your morality starts looking meaningless, because it was just an imposition from the outside.

It was because of fear that you were moral, or because of greed that you were moral. All your character looks cheap, because I teach you a totally different kind of life: characterless. Only in characterlessness is there freedom. And only in characterlessness does real character arrive--character that springs from your very source, is not imposed from the outside, is not imposed by the society, is not a kind of obedience but is a growth of freedom. It is a totally different thing, it happens only to people who are rebellious enough.

I don't teach you obedience, I teach you rebellion.

So naturally, your spirituality gone, your morality gone, your knowledge gone, all down the drain--suddenly you are standing there looking stupid, nude, ignorant, characterless, immoral, unspiritual. Now, what kind of disciplehood is this? Naturally, the question arises.

But, Niseema, this is the beginning. First I have to take all that you have away--so your burdened heart is unburdened, so all the garbage that you have gathered is thrown out and you are clean, left clean. In that cleanliness, in that purity, in that unburdening, you will start growing.

And that growth I am not going to give to you, it will happen to you. You are ready for it--just the garbage is too much and it doesn't allow you to grow. It is as if a rosebush has been covered by garbage--Vedas, Gitas, Koranas, Bibles, all garbage--and the rosebush is dying. I have to take all these books away. Soon the rosebush will start growing, and the day is not far off when you will see the first roses blooming.

I feel to be enjoying sensual pleasures and in general to be very hedonistic.

Beautiful. Enjoy. Because it is only through enjoying them that you will come to see the illusoriness of them--there is no other way. If I say they are illusory, Ikkyu says they are illusory, Buddha says they are illusory, they are not going to become illusory just because these people say so. You have to see it on your own.

Buddha has said again and again: Don't believe what I say, unless you have examined it, lived it, observed it, concluded it, on your own.

How can you know the illusoriness of these enjoyments unless you go into them? Go into them. Go into them as totally as possible, so sooner you can come out. Be a hedonist. By being a hedonist you will see that all pleasures bring pain, that each pleasure is followed by great pain. Slowly slowly, you will see that the pleasure and pain are two aspects of the same coin. You cannot get rid of pain unless you see this. Once you have seen that pleasure and pain are together, inevitably together....

There is no way to separate them. That's what we have been doing, down the ages--just trying to separate them. We want all the pleasures and we don't want any pain. And they are together, they come together. We want to avoid pain and we want to enjoy pleasure. But the pain comes.

When you see this happening again and again, one day the very experience will make you capable of dropping both. And the day one drops pleasure and pain both, what happens is called bliss. Great silence, great joy arises--which is not pleasure, remember, because it has the counterpart of pain in it. It is sheer joy, eternal joy. But it arises only when pleasure and pain both have been dropped.

And if you don't become a hedonist, if you don't experience its truth, then you will become a spiritual hedonist. Then you will think of the same joys--in paradise of course, not here, but of the same joys. You will hanker after the same women, the same men, the same wine--but in paradise. You will have to postpone a little bit, that's all.

Your saints are just the same as you--in fact more greedy than you, more hedonistic than you, but they are waiting for paradise. They will take their revenge there. They will see to it that you all suffer in hell, because you enjoyed on the earth and they suffered on the earth, so now they will be rewarded. They will have beautiful women in paradise, eternally young, with no perspiration, etcetera, etcetera. And rivers of wine. Wine is not sold in pubs in paradise--rivers. And there has never ever been any effort for prohibition. You can jump into rivers of wine, you can bathe in rivers of wine, you can drink as much as you want. And all kinds of food will be available, and with no fear of becoming fat. Nobody has ever heard--have you ever seen any fat angel? They never become fat; they go on eating and eating. And all their work consists of is jubilation, singing songs in the praise of the Lord, and fooling around.

These are your saints. Once they were saints sitting with long faces, now they are fooling in paradise.

Your saints are not against pleasure, they are only against the momentariness of it; remember it. They are only against the momentariness of it, because it is fleeting. So what is the point of running after it? They are waiting for permanent pleasure. They are real hedonists, more hedonistic than you.

So if you become spiritual, so-called spiritual, then you will be just waiting for your time, impatiently waiting for when paradise arrives and you can jump into all kinds of pleasures. You can explode, and you can explore all kinds of pleasures that you have denied to yourself on the earth.

This is not much different; the worldly and the other-worldly are not different, they are the same.

What I am trying to make you aware of here is not that you have to become hedonistic in the other world, or you have to become antagonistic to hedonism in this world. What I am trying here is to make you aware of the whole situation of life. If something in your unconscious hankers for pleasure, go into it-- that is the only way to go beyond it. Going through is the only way to go beyond. Don't repress.

So Niseema, be hedonistic, totally hedonistic. Enjoy all sensual pleasures--there is no fear about it, because they are all dream stuff. So if you are enjoying a dream, I am the last person to be worried about it. If your saints are against it, that simply shows that they have not yet understood that it is all a dream. Why should they be against it?

That's why my statements sometimes make you very much confused. Just the other day, I talked against love. And every night, every evening, I suggest to people to move into love. They become very puzzled. They have fallen in love with this madman-- in the morning he says "All love is illusion", in the evening he says "Fall in love, go headlong."

I am saying it because it is illusion: go headlong, so soon you will be out of it. If you go in a miserly way you may take years or lives to come out of it, and I may not be here to help you. So I say go headlong--just jump into the whole turmoil of the world, so that you can come out of the illusion. If it is an illusion you will come out of it, there is no need to be worried about it. And even if you don't come out of it, so what? It is just an illusion! Enjoy it while it lasts!

Sooner or later you are bound to be awake. And my own experience is that the more you go into these experiences of life, the more the awakening comes closer. When the night is darkest the morning is the closest. When you are moving in an illusion so deeply and it looks so real that everything else looks unreal in comparison to it, that is the moment when the morning is very close.

You say: This doesn't fit with my previous feelings and ideas about being close to a master.

How can you have any ideas without being close to a master? What expectations can you have? All those expectations will be your projections--will be your desires, your fears, your greed. They can't be based on truth.

Now you are with me. Being with me for a few years, you will know what it is to be with a master. If you can remain with me long enough to be finished totally, then you will know what it is to be with a master. It is to be with your own death, total death.

But only when you are annihilated is there a possibility of God arising in you. Only after crucifixion the door opens for resurrection.

The third question

A while ago, someone who is also past the age of fifty like me, said to me: You are still a disciple?

The person who said it is very self-reliant, self-sufficient. He does not look to others to find out what he should do. He is enough to himself.

I constantly look outside at others for more knowledge, for more skills. I am timid, diffident, and have little self-confidence. I am not enough to myself.

For me there are only these two stages: the disciple and the master. What is this third stage, the self-sufficient fully grown-up person that does not look for a master? Is this a deception?

THE FIRST THING TO BE UNDERSTOOD: you say, A while ago, someone who is also past the age of fifty like me, said to me: You are still a disciple?" Next time you meet him, say to him, "You are still not a disciple?"

What does being a disciple mean, in fact? It means that you have started learning. Instead of collecting knowledge, you have started learning. Disciplehood means you have found somebody who has known. You would like to meet and merge with this person's being, so you can also have some taste of reality.

There are egoistic people who would not like that, they would not like to meet and merge with anybody. They would like to remain sufficient unto themselves--even if it is hell. Even if they are suffering they will not show it to anybody. And they must be suffering, because ego is hell.

Disciplehood simply means that you are losing the boundaries of your ego. First you lose it with one person, and then you see the beauty of losing it. That's what happens with a master. You see the beauty of losing your boundaries, then you start losing it with everybody else too. Then one day you are capable of losing it with the whole existence.

A man who thinks that he is sufficient unto himself will never open up, will remain closed. He will live in what Soren Kierkegaard calls 'a shut-upness'. He will be a monad, windowless. He will suffer agonies, but he will think they are worth it because he has not to look to anybody, he is sufficient unto himself.

Once it happened, a chief minister of a state--and it will be better to call him a 'mischief minister'--came to see me, and he said, "I am a self-made man." I told him, "Thank you. You have relieved God of a great responsibility."

Self-made?

You have to be born out of a mother and a father. You have to depend for your breathing on the air, you have to depend for your food on the trees, you have to depend for your warmth on the sun. You have to depend on the seas, rivers, fire. You are dependent!

From where comes this nonsense: "I am self-made"? Can you exist even for a single moment if you are disconnected from everything you are plugged into?

Just think--disconnected from the sun! Think--disconnected from the air! Think--disconnected from the earth! Can you live? Can you exist even for a single moment? Impossible.

The idea that "I am sufficient unto myself", that "I am a self-made person", is just one of the most egoistic attitudes--foolish and false. We are not independent, we are not dependent; we live in a kind of interdependence, that is the truth. These two words are just two extremes--independence and dependence are two extremes. Both are false. Just exactly in the middle of the two is the truth: interdependence.

Because really the whole exists--I don't exist, you don't exist. How can I be self-sufficient? How can you be self-sufficient? Nobody can be. Only the whole is self-sufficient, and only the whole can be self-sufficient. The whole exists on its own. That's why we say God is self-sufficient--God means the total. God is not a person, but the totality of all. It includes everything--so it cannot depend on anything else, because there is nothing outside it.

But if you look inside, then each part depends on another. Then we live in an ocean of interdependence. You cannot be born without a mother, without a father. You cannot be born without existence supporting you from every side, visibly, invisibly.

When you are in love you cannot be self-sufficient, you will seek a woman or a man. When you meditate you will need somebody who knows what meditation is, not through books but through his experience.

That's what Ikkyu means when he says: Ask someone, ask the awakened. Ask someone who has mercy and sincerity, truth and wisdom. Ask somebody who has known, who has become. Ask somebody who has disappeared. Ask somebody who no more exists on the plane of ego, whose ego is no more relevant. Be with him, be in his presence, imbibe his presence.

And remember, you are not becoming dependent on another human being. That's why in the East we don't call the master a human being. We have called Buddha 'Bhagwan', Mahavira 'Bhagwan', Krishna 'Bhagwan', for a certain reason. We don't call them human beings. Not that they are not just like you--they are just like you, and yet something has happened in them that has transformed their being, has illuminated their being. Something of the beyond has penetrated them. They are openings to God, so we have called them gods.

Christians feel very offended, Mohammedans feel very offended, Jews feel very offended, when they think that Buddha is called a god. Why? He is just a human being--Buddha himself says, "I am a human being." But a human being who no more exists on the plane of the ego. Yes, just like you, he has the body. And he eats and excretes and sleeps and he is born and will die just like you. But still, something is there which is not like you: he is absent in the deepest core of his being. And through that absence a new presence has become available there: God has descended in him. You can have a look through him into the totality of all.

To find a master does not mean that you have contacted a person, it means you have contacted a presence. Just presence, not a person.

A while ago, someone who is also past the age of fifty like me, said to me: You are still a disciple? The person who said it is very self-reliant, self-sufficient.

He is missing a lot. He must be utterly bored.

He does not look to others to find out what he should do. He is enough to himself.

He will live a closed life. Help him to open up, help him to merge with the whole. And it is difficult to merge with the whole suddenly, it is too much to take in. You have to find a small door to enter.

When you start learning swimming you don't just go into the sea; you have to learn in shallow water by the banks or in a swimming pool.

A master is just a small door into the infinity of God. It is easier to enter from that door rather than jump into the sky directly. If one can jump into the sky directly it is perfectly good--but that type of man will never say, "I am self-sufficient." He cannot say it, because that type of person will know that there is no self. Jumping into the whole is losing the self. If somebody thinks, "I am self-sufficient and I never look up to anybody else," he is simply living his ego trip.

Help him to open up. And don't allow him to close you up. Because your ego must feel hurt--when somebody says, "You are fifty, and you are still a disciple?" your ego will feel hurt. You will think, "So I am looking to others."

The master is not the other. When you have fallen in tune with a master, he is not the other! He is more yourself than you are. That, only a disciple knows--he will laugh at the whole idea. If you ask Sariputra, "Is Buddha the other, someone that you look up to?" he will laugh. He will say, "There is nobody to look up to. He is more me than I am myself. He is my future, he is my potential, my possibility. He is my hope. Through him I have seen what I can be, what is my destiny. Through him I have become aware of the blooming flowers--they have bloomed in him, I am just a seed. He has given a glimpse of my own possibilities. He is me."

When a disciple is really a disciple, not just a student, then he will say, "The master and I are not two." And if there is ever a question of choosing, the disciple will choose the master, not himself. Because the master is closer to his being than he himself is.

I constantly look outside at others for more knowledge, for more skills. I am timid, diffident, and have little self-confidence.

That is far better than having so-called self-confidence.

Because with self-confidence, confidence is just a shadow; the real thing is the self. There is no self--how can there be self-confidence?

A real man, a man who has known, lives without self, lives without self-confidence. Not that he lives in a kind of no-confidence--with confidence disappearing, unconfidence also disappears. He simply lives, not bothering about confidence or no-confidence. He simply lives. He is unworried, because the whole has taken care. He has surrendered to the whole, now the whole knows better. He simply flows with the whole--wherever it is going, he is also going. He is in a surrender.

You are in a far better state than your friend. People come to me and they ask, "How to gain more self-confidence?" For what? Just to make this self look strong? Just to compete with others, fight with others? to prove yourself, that you are greater than others? For what?

Lose the self too! Lose self-confidence, lose self. Let then go, they are all diseases. You just relax into non-being.

And remember, I am not saying that the man of non-being is un-self-confident. He simply lives, like the trees are living. Do you think any tree is self-confident? or un-self-confident? Do you think any river is self-confident or un-self-confident? The whole question is irrelevant; you cannot ask that question, it is pointless, it is meaningless.

The trees flow, grow. The rivers flow, grow. Things are happening. There is nobody taking care of everything. To surrender to this happening is to disappear as an ego. And great joy arises with that surrender.

For me there are only these two stages: the disciple and the master. What is this third stage, the self-sufficient fully grown-up person that does not look for a master?

The fully grown person is not a person at all. The moment you are fully grown you become a presence, not a person--the person disappears. All persons are immature; personality is immaturity. To be a person means to be false. The word 'person' comes from 'persona', mask--it is a mask, it is just a face that you have put on yourself to show others. this is not your reality. No person can ever become mature or grown-up, Because no mask can ever be grown-up. The mask hinders.

Drop the mask! Forget about the person! Then presence arises. A presence with no self, with no center in it. A pure presence, just a light. And then life is lived in totality, in celebration.

You ask me: The self-sufficient fully grown-up person--is this a deception?

Yes. 'Person' is a deception, and 'fully grown-up' is an absolute deception. All personalities are ungrown-up, all personalities are childish. Presence is grown-upness, maturity. And to be with a master is to be with a presence. To be with a presence is slowly slowly moving towards the presence, and one day you will also become aflame.

One day when you come really close to a master, something jumps from the master into you--a flame. Just as it happens when you bring an unlit candle very close to a lit candle. Just a moment before, the unlit candle was unlit and the lit candle was lit. And just a moment afterwards, at a certain distance the flame jumps and both the candles are lit. And the lit candle has not lost anything, and the unlit has gained all.

The master never loses anything. That's why millions of disciples can become lit through a single master. But there is nothing like a fully self-sufficient grown-up person; that is just a deception.

There is a fully grown-up presence. A flame, a light.

The last question

You say that it is important to have courage and sincerity. Therefore I will drop my fear and ask you the questions deepest and most honestly within me, and I hope you will answer. How can there be any generalizations about the qualities of man and woman? We are each and every one of us fifty percent man and fifty percent woman, then we must each possess varying degrees of male or female characteristics not dependent entirely on if our physical bodies in this lifetime are born male or female. I am female but I have always written poetry and I have never been so good at shopping lists. I am female but I have not been suspicious or jealous of man's love affair with his art. In fact I have more often been in the role of choosing to be with my writing, than choosing to be in relationship leading to home and family. I am female but I feel my creativity and ideas come from strongly within me, and do not look to a man for them. If I have been uncertain about my wholeness within, I have looked outside but never specifically to someone because of the sex they happen to be.

And I have loved women as well as men--not when no man was available to me, but because I was not looking at the outer illusion of this being man or woman, but feeling the essence of that person within. I feel these generalizations reinforce our already strong preoccupation with the world of illusion and belief in the physical universe. You can see you've made me angry, so I suppose you have begin to reach me.

The question is from Sky Deborah.

THE FIRST THING: generalizations are generalizations. They are not applicable to every single particular human being, that's why they are called generalizations. The average man does not exist, you cannot find the average man anywhere. But the idea is good, it helps clarity. You cannot find, absolutely corresponding to the generalized idea, a single human being. Human beings come in all sizes and shapes and colours, they are unique. But still, generalization has its own point....

For example, only one single woman has asked the question-- there are thousands of women here. Secondly, the very question shows me that Deborah must be very good at making shopping lists. And I am afraid about her poetry too. You can write a shopping list in poetry form. I would have to have a look at her poetry, only then can I say anything.

My own experience is that out of a hundred poetries ninety-nine are shopping lists. It does not matter whether they are written by men or women. It is very rare to find poetry.

It is said of a great Zen master, Lin Chi.... He had ten thousand monks, disciples, in his monastery. The king had come to see the monastery, he was very much impressed, and Lin Chi was taking him around. And the king asked, "How many disciples do you have?" He said, "One in a hundred."

A strange answer--one in a hundred? But that's how it has always been. When you have a hundred disciples only one is really a disciple. Ninety-nine are just hangers-around.

Even a great poet, when he writes poetry, ninety-nine times writes only shopping lists. Only once in a while the poetry happens--all poetries are not poetic. And sometimes this too happens, that a shopping list may have great poetry. All shopping lists are not necessarily unpoetic.

But Deborah must belong to the new kind of woman that is arising in the world, the lib woman.

One thing has to be understood: the liberation movement that is going on in the world is a man-created phenomenon, a male-created phenomenon. You will be surprised about it, that it is again a male conspiracy. Now man wants to get rid of women. He wants to have no responsibility. He wants to enjoy women but only as fun; he does not want to take all the other responsibilities that come with it.

Now, this is a subtle conspiracy: the man is trying to persuade women all over the world that the woman has to become independent. It is a subtle trick. And the male mind is cunning and the male mind is succeeding. And now many women have become poisoned by this idea.

Do you know? The first persons who started talking about equality between man and woman were men, not women. The first persons who started talking about it, that they should have equal freedom, were men, not women. The seed comes from the male mind. And it has always been so--whenever a man feels what is in his favour, he manages it. His cunning is very subtle. And sometimes he manages it in such a way that the woman thinks she is doing it on her own.

In the past also it has been so. Man has persuaded women in the past that they are pure beings, angels. Man is dirty, boys are boys--but the woman? She is divine. Man has put woman on a high pedestal; that was his trick to control woman. Man has worshipped, and through worship he has controlled. And naturally, when the woman was on the pedestal she thought that she was something divine--she could not do those things that men are doing, she could not, because that was going against her ego. That high pedestal was very ego-satisfying. She was the mother, she was divine; she had more divine qualities than man. Man is ugly, immoral, and all that. Man has to be forgiven for that.

So man, down the ages, started remaining in his ways. And the woman was high. But this was a trick, the ego was persuaded. And once your ego is persuaded, you are caught. Then you cannot move from your posture. To ask for equality will be a kind of fall-- you will have to come down to become equal. It was a strategy, and the woman followed it. She remained pure, she remained virgin up to the marriage.

It was not so for the man. If the woman died, the man was allowed to marry again--because boys are boys, they cannot live without the woman. If the man died, the woman had to remain a widow for her whole life. Or, in this country particularly--which did this strategy to the very logical end--she had to commit suicide. She had to burn herself alive with the husband. And millions of women did it. How were they persuaded? And do you think they were forced? No, nobody was forcing them.

There was no visible coercion, just a very deep seduction. By becoming *satis*, by going into the fire with the husband, their egos were fulfilled. Greatly fulfilled--people worshipped them. When they entered into the fire, thousands of people would gather together and sing songs in praise of the purity of woman.

And if a woman did not go with the husband into the fire, did not commit suicide, she was condemned, utterly condemned. She was a bad woman. Just by trying to be alive, she was a bad woman. She was disrespected; she would fall immediately in the eyes of others, she would lose all respect. Her life would become a hell. She would be condemned everywhere, she would not be welcomed anywhere. She would be thought of as a bad omen.

In no marriage would she be able to participate. If a child was born and people were celebrating, she would not be able to participate. She would not be allowed to decorate her body, to use beautiful clothes or ornaments or have long hair--no, she had to live in an ugliness, and condemned from everywhere. It was worse than life, worse than death. So it was better to jump into the fire once and for all, and have the respect.

And temples were raised in the memory of those women. And those women were thinking that they were doing it. What I am making clear is that those women down the ages were thinking that they were doing it, on their own. And it was not so.

Now again the same is happening, in the reverse order. In the West, man has persuaded women that "Now you have to be free, you have to be equal." Because now things have changed, times have changed--a man would like to enjoy more women than just his wife. Now he wants absolute freedom. And the only way to have absolute freedom is to give absolute freedom to the woman.

And he has persuaded her again. And now the woman protesters and libbers, they are shouting with their whole heart for liberty and equality. And they don't know they are again in the same grip: again man is persuading them. Now man wants to use them and throw them, with no responsibility attached to it.

If you look deeply into the whole matter of it, you will be surprised. The male mind is a cunning mind. The woman is more innocent; she cannot be so strategic, so political, she has always believed the man. And you will be surprised: these lib women are again believing in the man! Nothing has changed. Now this is in favour of the man that you should be free and you should not ask for any commitment. He does not want to commit himself, he wants to have all freedom. He does not want to take the responsibility of your children. He does not want to live with you for ever, he wants to change his woman every day.

But now again he is creating beautiful words: One should live in no commitment. One should live without involvement. One should not be possessive, one should not be jealous. Now again he is creating beautiful philosophy. He has done it before too--and then too women were deceived, and again they are going to be deceived. Women trust. Trust is easy for them; love comes easier to them than logic. And they are very much concerned with the immediate. The man always thinks of strategies, tactics, what will happen, how it will happen--he thinks of the future, he plans for the future.

Now, Deborah repeats at least five times in this question: I am a female.

Is there some worry? Is there some doubt? There must be. One thing has to be told to you: just by being in a female body one need not be a woman. Just by being in a male body one need not be a man. Man and woman are more states of the mind. There are men who are psychologically not male but female, and there are women who are psychologically not women but men. These are the people who create many problems, because they cannot be heterosexual. Heterosexuality has no appeal for them, they have to be homosexuals or lesbians. Their psychology is different from their physiology; their biology and their psychology have a gap in them, unbridged.

And there is going to remain a problem with them. In fact in a better world, in the future world--soon, I think by the end of this century--things will be easier. Because if a man is deep down psychologically feeling himself a woman, it is better to go through an operation and become biologically also a woman. Or if a woman is feeling deep down a male, it is better to go through an operation, plastic surgery, and become a man, so it can be bridged.

Once this becomes possible, homosexuality and lesbianism will disappear from the world. Otherwise it cannot disappear, because it has a certain reason in it. The man looks a man from the outside; deep down he is not a man, he is a woman. His deeper woman wants a man--hence the homosexual.

And there is a third category also: confused people, who don't know who they are. In the morning they are women, by the evening they are men. The difference is so small that they shrink; they become bisexuals. One moment they are loving a woman, another moment they are falling in love with a man. Their psychology and biology is in a state of mess; they will live a very confused life. Science can now help these people too, to make things clear.

Now, repeating again and again that "I am a female" creates suspicion. Why so much concern about being a female? Once would have been enough. Even once was not needed--your question would have said that you are a female. And not an ordinary female, a libber.

Let me read the question: You say that it is important to have courage and sincerity. Therefore I will drop my fear and ask you the questions deepest and most honestly within me...

Now, what kind of questions are deepest and honest in you?

Just think of the whole crap of it. These are the deepest questions? I am talking about Ikkyu and Buddha, and these are the deepest questions. And to ask these questions you needed great courage and sincerity!

How can there be any generalizations about the qualities of man and woman?

Generalizations are not possible about anything, because no individual will fit them. But still, generalizations are meaningful; they simply indicate. When I say a woman is more concerned with the immediate, I am not saying anything about a particular woman--Deborah, or anybody else. I am simply saying it about womanness, that womanness is concerned with the immediate. And if you are not concerned with the immediate then something somewhere in your womanhood is missing. That is very essential to femininity: the concern for the immediate, the imminent.

But generalizations are generalizations, remember it. And there will be differences between individuals. But the meaning of a generalization is just to indicate a certain quality. It doesn't say anything about particular individuals, it simply says the quality of being a woman is immediateness.

I would like to see Deborah's poetry, because there is a possibility there may be that immediateness in the poetry itself. The poetry may be concerned with the imminent, the herenow; it may not be concerned with the ultimate. And the question also shows it--her whole concern is her womanhood. She says, "This is my deepest and the most honest question arising in me."

Buddhahood, God, they are faraway questions. Her whole concern is with her body, her womanhood. It is not just an accident that women are standing before the mirror for hours. Their concern is immediate; they are more concerned with the body than with the soul. They are more materialistic than spiritualistic. They are more factual than fictitious.

I am a female but I have always written poetry and I have never been so good at shopping lists. I am female but I have not been suspicious or jealous of man's love affair with his art. In fact, I have more often been in the role of choosing to be with my writing, than choosing to be in relationship leading to home and family.

Now, these are complex things. The atmosphere is such that a woman has to be equal with man. She has not to be interested in the home, family, children, motherhood. She has to become interested in poetry, in literature, in painting, in science, in technology, this and that. Now women's groups gather together around the world to raise their consciousness. And all their consciousness-raising sessions consist of only one thing, that they have to destroy something deep in their womanhood. Only then can they compete with men.

They are soft, naturally soft. They cannot compete with men. If they want to compete with men they will have to become hard. So whenever you come across a lib woman you can see the face loses softness. It is very difficult to say to a lib woman, "Baby"-- very difficult. And she will be angry too, she will not like it. Why 'Baby'?--she is equal to you. Hardness arises.

All kinds of struggle give hardness. And you may be trying not to be interested in the home, because if you become interested in the home then you cannot compete in the world. If you become interested in children you cannot compete in the world; then that becomes a distraction. And if you have to compete in the world and prove that you are as strong as men, you have to somehow become more like men.

And this will be a loss. This is a loss--because the only hope for humanity is the softness of woman, not the hardness of man. We have suffered enough from the hardness of man. What is needed is that man should become more like woman, rather than woman becoming more like man.

Nietzsche is right when he says that Buddha and Christ were a little womanish. I agree. And this is how it should be--because Buddha is the hope. Men should become a little more womanish, more soft, more waterlike. But what is happening is very unfortunate, women are trying to become like men. Naturally, with whomsoever you compete, you try to become like that. If you are antagonistic against men, sooner or later you will become more like men.

Women are pulling against themselves, trying hard to manage. But that is not natural. The natural is the womb in the woman--that womb hankers for a child, that womb hankers for a home. The home is the visible womb outside the woman, it is a projection of the inner womb.

Once a woman is no more interested in the home, she is no more interested in her womb. And that womb is there. And men and women are not equal, because man is missing that womb. How can they be equal? I am not saying they are unequal, but I am certainly saying they are not equal. They are so different--how can they be equal? They are polar opposites. They are so different, they cannot be compared in terms of equality or inequality. A woman is a woman, a man is a man. And they should remain man and woman. A woman should remain interested in the home, because once she stops being interested in the home she will stop being interested in the womb, in the child. And then naturally she turns into a lesbian.

It is not accidental that libbers become lesbians. Because if you are not interested in the womb and not interested in the child, then for what be interested in men? Then it is good to be interested in women. This is a very strange phenomenon that is happening in the world.

My own understanding is this, that man has to become a little more feminine. He has gone too far away in becoming a man, he has lost track of all humanity. Don't follow him, don't compete with him--otherwise you will be going on in the same rut, in the same routine. You will become warlike. And the libbers screaming and shouting and protesting on the streets are just ugly. They are showing the worst traits of the male mind.

And the last thing: You can see you have made me angry, so I suppose you have begun to reach me.

Now I must have made you even more angry. Fall in love with me!

THIS MOUNTAIN ECHO

Whatever runs counter
To the mind and will of ordinary people
Hinders the Law of Men
And the Law of Buddha.

I would like
To offer you something,
But in the Daruma Sect
We have nothing at all.

As Ikkyu does not think of his body
As if it were his body,
He lives in the same place,
Whether it is town or country.

The mind of man is without sound,
Without odour;
He who answers when called
Is nothing but a thief.

If we say "There is,"
People think "There is";
But though it answers,
It is not,
This mountain echo.

If we say, "There is not,"
People think "There is not,"
Though it answers,
The mountain echo.

A parable:

A KING WANTED TO PICK THE WISEST MAN among his subjects to be his prime minister.

When the search finally narrowed down to three men, he decided to put them to the supreme test. Accordingly, he placed them in a room in his palace, and installed a lock which was the last word in mechanical ingenuity. The candidates were informed that whoever was able to open the door first would be appointed to the post of honour.

The three men immediately set themselves to the task. Two of them at once began to work out complicated mathematical formulas to discover the proper lock-combination. The third man, however, just sat in his chair doing nothing. Finally, without bothering to put pen to paper, he got up, walked to the door, turned the knob, and the door opened. It had been unlocked all the time!

THIS IS THE SITUATION. Nothing is locked, the door is open. And people are pondering upon ways and means to unlock the lock. People are trying different methodologies, practising a thousand and one things, to get out. And in fact they are out. Unless they stop this thinking business they will not know the truth of the situation.

Man is not in bondage, only thinks so. Because he thinks so, he is in bondage. There is no difference between a Buddha and an ordinary man. But the ordinary man thinks there is a difference--then there is.

You create your prisons, your locks. And then you try to find out the ways to get out of them.

Buddhism cuts the knot with one stroke. Buddhism says: There is no lock, no knot to cut. That's what I mean when I say Buddhism cuts the knot with one stroke of the sword. There is nowhere to go, nothing to be done. You are already there, and you are already that: just open your eyes. Think of those two great thinkers--they must have been mathematicians, they must have been engineers--naturally they inferred that the lock must be of great mechanical ingenuity and they had to find the proper combination. They started working.

Now, they can go on working for eternity--do you think they will ever find a solution? There is no possibility of any solution, because the problem does not exist in the first place.

In fact they will get more and more entangled. They will get more and more entangled--not in the problem, because there is no problem, but in the answers that they will invent.

That's where people are stuck. Somebody is a Hindu, he is stuck with his answer. Somebody is a Christian, he is stuck with his answer. People are stuck in philosophies, and no philosophy is needed. Life is enough unto itself. It needs no elaboration, it needs no explanation, it needs no analysis.

But if you become part of an analytic game then it can go on and on for ever. One thing will lead to another, and that to another, and you are in a chain. And because the problem will never be solved, because there is no problem to be solved, you will have to go on looking for the answers.

Buddhism brings you down to the earth. It says: First look to see whether the lock is locked, whether there is any lock on the door.

There is none. The door is open.

How can there be a lock on the door of existence? We are part of it--who is going to lock it? for what? Who is going to create the problem? and for what? We are existence: we are in it, it is in us. Seeing this, one relaxes. In that relaxation, the vision arises.

That's what happened to the third man. He was not pondering, thinking, analyzing, inventing, inferring. He simply sat there in the chair doing nothing. That's what meditation is all about.

The English word 'meditation' is not a right word, because in English 'meditation' also means 'to think about, to meditate upon'. English has no right word for *dhyana* to be translated, because *dhyana* exactly means 'not to meditate upon', *dhyana* exactly means 'not to think upon'. *Dhyana* means not to do anything, just relax and be.

When you are just silent and doing nothing, your perspective is infinite, your perception is clear, you can see through and through. Sitting silently in the chair doing nothing, the man could see that there was no lock on the door. He simply went up, turned the knob and went out.

This is my experience too. This parable is not just a parable, not an invented parable. It is the parable of all the Buddhas: this is how it is. This is not just an invented story; it is the condensed experience, the most essential experience of all the Buddhas--that there is no lock on the door. You just sit silently, attain to a state of seeing, of purity, of no thought disturbing, of no cloud of thought moving around your consciousness--just the clean mirror with no dust of thought--and suddenly you will be able to see that there is no lock, no door, no enemy, no death, no birth. And you are not to go anywhere and you are not to become somebody.

You are perfect as you are. You are already in that space called paradise. Start enjoying it, don't make a problem out of it. The moment you create a problem out of it, you stop enjoying. How can you enjoy unless you solve the problem. And one problem creates ten problems...ad nauseam.

Cut the first problem! Life is not a problem. Buddha says: Life is simple.

I have heard:

A king went into his garden and found wilted and dying trees, shrubs and flowers. The oak said it was dying because it could not be tall like the pine. Turning to the pine, he found it drooping because it was unable to bear grapes like the vine. And the vine was dying because it could not blossom like the rose. He found heartsease blooming and as fresh as ever. Upon inquiry, he received this reply:

"I took it for granted that when you planted me you wanted heartsease. If you had desired an oak, a vine or a rose, you would have planted them. So I thought, since you had put me here, I should do the best I can to be what you want. I can be nothing but what I am, and I am trying to be that to the best of my ability."

The heartsease is saying what Buddha has said. You are here because this existence needs you as you are. Otherwise somebody else would have been here!--the existence would not have helped you to be here, would not have created you. You are fulfilling something very essential, something very fundamental, as you are.

And your so-called mahatmas go on teaching you, "Become a Buddha, become a Christ, become a Krishna." Nobody tells you just to be yourself. Why should you become a Buddha? If God wanted a Buddha he could have produced as many Buddhas as he wanted. He produced only one Buddha, and that was enough. And he was satisfied to his heart's desire, utterly satisfied. Since then he has not produced another Buddha or another Christ. He has created you instead. Just think of the respect that the universe has given to you. You have been chosen!--not Buddha, not Christ, not Krishna.

You will be needed more, that's why. You fit more now. Their work is done, they contributed their fragrance to existence. Now you have to contribute your fragrance.

But the moralists, the puritans, the priests, they go on teaching you, they go on driving you crazy. They say to the rose, "Become a lotus." And they say to the lotus, "What are you doing here? You have to become something else." They drive the whole garden crazy, everything starts dying--because nobody can be anybody else, that is not possible. The rose is a rose and the lotus is a lotus. And the lotus is good as a lotus, it can live only as a lotus. If it tries to be a rose it will die, it will become paralyzed--that is not possible because that is not intrinsic to it; that cannot arise.

And if the lotus really becomes a victim of the priests and starts trying to be a rose, or the rose tries to be a lotus, what is going to happen? The lotus will become pseudo; as a lotus it will start dying, and as a rose it will pretend.

That's what has happened to humanity. Everybody is pretending. Authenticity is lost, truth is lost, everybody is trying to show that he is somebody else. Just look at yourself: you are pretending to be somebody else. And you can be only yourself-- there is no other way, there has never been, there is no possibility that you can be anybody else. You will remain yourself. You can enjoy it and bloom, or you can wither away if you condemn it. Humanity looks so ugly, for this simple reason.

A matchmaker was asked by a young artist to find him a suitable mate. "I know just the girl for a creative man like you!" cried the marriage-broker.

The next day the matchmaker brought the girl to the artist's house. The young man was shocked with her appearance and at the first opportunity he drew the broker aside.

"What kind of a monster do you call that?" he hissed.

"One eye slanted up, the other down; the left ear way up here, the right ear way down there; the forehead sloped back like a..."

"Look, you're an artist," interrupted the matchmaker. "You should know better than anyone else--you either like Picasso or you don't!"

And every man on this earth has become a Picasso, a perversion. Beauty is lost--because beauty always follows integrity, beauty is a shadow of an integrated presence. You are disintegrated, you are divided against yourself. You are a rose and trying to be a lotus, a marigold trying to be a rose, an oak trying to be a pine. You are divided, you are fighting with yourself.

This fight is destroying your joy, this fight is dissipating your energies, this fight is suicidal. Don't kill yourself any more! Just drop fighting, and start living. This very moment it can be dropped.

But why can you not drop it? Why are these priests really so influential? There must be some reason in you too. The reason is that their idea that you should become this and that, helps your ego. If you listen to the Buddha or if you listen to me, it will not help your ego at all. Then you are simply what you are: relax and live. Then you are ordinary. Then how are you going to be somebody special?

And the ego hankers for speciality, the ego is always trying to be somebody in particular. And these Zen people say: Eat when you are hungry. And this looks so ordinary. And the priests say: Fast when you are hungry. That looks special, that looks extraordinary--something to do, something to be. When everybody is just an ordinary eater, you are fasting. It gives you a haughtiness, it gives you a great feeling of the ego: you are special, you are not ordinary.

When everybody is enjoying, the priests say, "Live with a long face, only then can you attain to God." That appeals to you. When everybody is dancing, singing--and that's what life is, a dance and a song--the priests say, "Go to the Himalayas and sit silently in a cave with closed eyes watching your navel." That appeals.

Just watch! You are attracted by things which are outlandish, unnatural--because only outlandish and unnatural things, bizarre things, can give you the feeling that you are special. And trying to be special, you will never be able to know what is. You will be so much concerned with being special and somebody, you will not be able to live and love and to see and to understand and to be.

The famous sage seemed to be fast asleep. Nearby sat some of his followers. They carried on a whispered conversation about the sage's unparalleled virtues.

"What generosity!" exclaimed one. "There isn't another one like him in all the land."

"And his piety is without limit!" exclaimed a second.

"And his education!" cried a third. "He's a real genius."

"And his patience! He never gets excited."

They fell silent for a minute. Whereupon the sage slowly opened one eye and said, "And my modesty you don't even mention!"

This is how things are, everybody wants to be special. All the nonsense that goes on in the name of religion and spirituality is nothing but ego decoration.

A really religious man is bound to be very ordinary. This is the refrain of Ikkyu's sutras today.

Whatever runs counter
To the mind and will of ordinary people
Hinders the Law of Men
And the Law of Buddha.

A GREAT STATEMENT. A rare statement. only a man who knows can say such a thing. It can't be uttered by the pundits and the scholars, it can be said only by a seer. It has the taste that one has known, that one has lived, that one has experienced. It is a rebellious statement. Just think of its implications: "Whatever runs counter to the mind and will of ordinary people is against the Law of Buddha." So whatsoever is in tune with the ordinary mind, with the ordinary people, is in tune with the Law of Buddha.

See the immensity of the implications. Don't try to be special-- because the only way to be special is to run counter to the ordinary man. If the ordinary man is interested in sex, you be interested in celibacy--run counter. If the ordinary man is interested in eating and drinking and merrying, you drop all those. If the ordinary man is interested in small things, you simply remain interested in great things--God, nirvana, moksha, truth. If the ordinary man lives in the marketplace, you go to a monastery.

Just do the reverse, that is the only way to be special. If the ordinary man simply stands on his feet, you stand on your head, do *sirshasana*. If the ordinary man feels good to lie down in a comfortable bed, you make a bed of thorns. If the ordinary man wants his body to be beautiful, you make your body ugly, you destroy its grace. If the ordinary man is doing something, then just to be counter to it, just to be against it, is your religion. And that's what religion is not feasting but fasting. That's what religion has become.

But this is not the true religion--not the religion of the Buddhas, of those who know. Ikkyu is saying:

Whatever runs counter
To the mind and will of ordinary people
Hinders the Law of Men
And the Law of Buddha.

What is the Law of Men and the Law of Buddha? What is Tao, what is Dhamma? To be just natural, easy. To be that which you are, with no hankering to be somebody else. Just see the point: great joy arises then. Of course nobody will know you, nobody will know that you are a great historical person. Nobody will know that you are of those few people who make or mar history. Nobody may ever know about you--not even your wife may know, or your husband or your children--because you will be simple and you will be living your life naturally.

Who knows about a rosebush that blooms? Nobody takes note of it in history. Nobody will take note of you either, but there is no need. History is the concern of the foolish people, fame is the concern of the foolish people, name is the concern of the foolish people.

The really wise person is not interested in fame, name, etcetera. He simply lives the moment: Sometimes he becomes famous, but that is another matter. Buddha became famous but he was not trying to; there was no desire. If he becomes, it is okay; if he does not become, it is okay. It is all okay, it is always okay. His flavour is that of okayness, everything is okay.

Enjoy your food, enjoy your bath, enjoy the sun, enjoy the wind and the rains, and enjoy everything that is available to you. And just remain whosoever you are--true to yourself, creating no hypocrisy, creating no pretension, creating no facade, no face. And utter joy will be yours, God will be yours. God comes only to those who are in an utter relaxation with their being. And the person who longs for something cannot be relaxed, because that longing creates tension.

Whatever runs counter
To the mind and will of ordinary people...

Just see the ordinary people. But it is very difficult to find ordinary people, very difficult, because everybody has become extraordinary. It is very difficult to find a sane person, because everybody has become insane. Centuries of priests, mahatmas and saints have driven everybody out of his soul, out of his home.

There are only neurotic people on the earth. Friedrich Nietzsche is reported to have said that everybody is neurotic--and if you think you are not, then that must be another kind of neurosis. But everybody is neurotic.

What is neurosis? Not being happy with yourself is neurosis, not being contented with yourself is neurosis. And then you get into turmoil and trouble. Then you lose all peace of mind, all joy of life. Then you exist in anguish, then you create hell for yourself.

Become ordinary. That's my teaching too, if it can be called a teaching--because up to now, teachings have been to drive you towards some extraordinary goal. But if you ask the awakened, they have always been saying: Just be ordinary. Don't strive. Live effortlessly, live in a let-go. And then nature takes possession of you. Your life becomes spontaneous, you live moment-to-moment--with no ideology to follow, with no conclusions. You live without conclusions; each moment brings its own reality and you respond to it. And you respond out of your total being--every cell of your body and mind and soul is involved in it.

Then you never repent--because how can you repent? You responded totally, so whatsoever happens is okay, because nothing else was possible. You had done all--you responded totally, you took the challenge. You can't repent if you live spontaneously. The people who repent are the people who live through conclusions. Then one mind says "Do this", another mind says "Do that"--because they have heard so many mahatmas and they have read so many books and they have listened to so many ideologies and so many teachers, and all those things are roaming around their minds, trying to impose themselves on the mind.

You choose one thing against something else. If you fail, then that something else which you had denied will take revenge with a vengeance. It will come back to the mind and will make you repent. It will say, "I have been telling you, choose me. And you were a fool to have chosen the other. Now remember in future." And you take a vow: "Then now I will listen to you." You repent.

But you have not understood yet. Repentance will always come if your decision is partial. And no decision lived out of conclusions can ever be total, because the conclusion has been carried from the past, and the situation is new--how can it fit totally? You have to respond again out of your newness of this moment, then the response is total. And total response is joy--whether it fails or succeeds, is irrelevant. In its totality it has succeeded already, and there will be no repentance.

Walt Whitman says, "Only what nobody denies is true." Just

listen to your innermost core, your ordinary nature, and you will know what truth is. The Christian denies the Hindu, the Hindu denies the Mohammedan, the Mohammedan denies the Christian, and they go on fighting and arguing. But look at the ordinary natural man, he is neither Christian nor Hindu. When he feels hungry he eats--and that is true for a Christian and that is true for a Hindu and that is true for a Mohammedan. Nobody denies it: this is truth.

When you feel tired you fall asleep--nobody denies it. This is truth. Truth is simple. Theories are complex and complicated. Theoreticians go on arguing, truth remains unargued.

Don't listen to what people say, listen to what they are. And you will be surprised--there is no difference between a Hindu and a Mohammedan and a Christian and a Jew, no difference at all. They go to different churches, obviously, and they read different books, certainly--but look into their nature. When it is hot the Hindu perspires as much as the Mohammedan; that is natural. The Mohammedan cannot say, "I am not a Hindu, and Hindus are perspiring. I cannot perspire, not at least now; that will be agreeing with the Hindus." When it is cold the body shivers--the body knows not whether it is a Christian or a Jew or a Jain; it shivers. Just watch natural things, look into nature. And slowly slowly, you will understand Dhamma--the real religion, the Law of Buddhas.

Ikkyu says:

Hinders the Law of Men
And the Law of Buddha.

That too is tremendously important. He makes it equivalent--the Law of Men and the Law of Buddha are not two different things. For Ikkyu there is no other world, this is the only world, and the other world is hidden in it: you have to search in it to find it. You are not to renounce it--renouncing it, both will be renounced.

Zen people have a tremendous saying: "Samsara is nirvana". This world is that world, and there is no distinction between this and that, and that is not higher and this is not lower. The Law of Men and the Law of Buddha are the same law, looked at from different angles. It may be difficult for you to understand the Law of Buddha but you can understand the Law of Men--and follow that law, fall in tune with it.

Just live for a few days naturally. And you will be surprised that all that you have been thinking is far away starts happening so close by. You will be surprised that the God that you used to think is very very far away and will take millions of lives to reach, starts happening to you in your breathing, in the beat of your heart. God starts pulsating in your blood. He is already pulsating there, but you are far away--you don't give any attention to the close-by.

Nature means that which is here. Fall in tune with it. Never listen to anything that creates a dichotomy between you and nature: let this be a deciding factor, a criterion. Always judge things on this criterion, this is a touchstone. If something is proved on this touchstone then it is gold--otherwise throw it. If anybody is trying to tell you to become unnatural, avoid him! His appeal is to your ego, and he is driving you neurotic and he must have some investment in your neurosis.

There are people who live on people's neuroses, there are people who live on other people's madnesses. The priest lives on that, he has lived down the ages on that--a subtle exploitation of the helplessness of man. And he makes man more and more helpless, because he knows that only if man is helpless is he then in his power.

Avoid anything that makes you afraid of your nature, avoid each and everything that makes you condemn your nature--because the Law of Men is the Law of Buddha. And if you can read the book of nature inside you, you have all the Bibles and all the Korans and all the Vedas there; you need not consult anything else, your real master is there. And the real master always throws you there.

That's what Ikkyu is doing.

The truth of human beings is the only truth there is. By finding that truth, you will know the truth of the trees and the rocks and the rivers too--because there are not many truths, there is only one truth. But that truth can be approached only through nature. There is no way to approach it by being unnatural, artificial, plastic.

A snob walked into a doctor's office and said, "Doctor, I feel terrible. I want you to give me a thorough examination and tell me what is wrong with me."

"Fine," said the doctor. "But first let me ask you a few questions. Do you drink much liquor?"

"I have never touched the vile stuff," the man replied indignantly.

"Do you smoke?" the doctor continued his inquiry.

"I have never touched the filthy weed."

"Do you run around much at night?"

"Of course not! I am in bed every night by ten o'clock for a good night's rest."

"Tell me," the doctor continued, "do you have sharp pains in the head?"

"That's just it!" the snob replied. "I have sharp pains in the head."

"That's the trouble, my dear man," the doctor advised. "Your halo is on too tight!"

Avoid these people with tight halos, avoid the people who have the look of holier-than-thou. They are the poisoners, they are the real enemies. But they are very influential--and their influence consists in giving you new props for your ego. If you can avoid anything that makes you unnatural, sooner or later you are bound to stumble upon the truth: the door is open! But these people are telling you complex theories about the lock and how to find the right combination. And they are arguing amongst themselves, because each thinks that he has found the right combination.

Nobody has opened the door, they are all inside--but arguing, convincing each other, converting each other. The foolishness of it... A Christian missionary converting Hindus into Christians, without being worried that he has not opened the door himself. Or a Hindu trying to convert a Christian to become Hindu, not thinking at all that he is wasting his time, he is still a prisoner. What is their joy? Their joy is also of the ego: "How many followers have I got? How many people believe in Christianity?" The number grows, and the ego grows with it. His ego is involved in the numbers. And your ego is strengthened, nourished, by anything that you do against nature.

Have you ever respected anybody for being natural? Just see the craziness of it--you always respect a person if he is unnatural.

Somebody was brought to me--a few followers came with him and they said, "Our guru is a great man. He eats only once in three days." Will you respect a man if he eats twice every day? I asked those people, "Will you respect your guru if he eats twice every day?" And the guru was almost starved, almost dying. But they are interested in something special--their guru is special, he eats only once in three days.

I came across a man, he has thousands of followers, because for ten years he has not slept. He is a raving maniac--bound to be so. Just don't sleep for ten days and you will know. And because of the fear that if he sits down or lies down he will fall asleep, for ten years he has been standing! He needs support on crutches, and people support him in the night and they go on doing kirtan the whole night so it keeps him awake--fully blasting loud-speakers. And they are killing this man! But they are happy that they have found the true master, he is happy because he has found the true followers. And both are utterly stupid. His face has no sign of any intelligence. How could an intelligent man fall into such a trap? But the ego is fulfilled. Now the fear is that if he drops it, then all his following will disappear. They are not really following him, they are following because he is doing something unnatural.

Down the ages, people have been doing unnatural things. And

you have been respecting unnatural things; you always respect unnatural things. If you respect anything unnatural, that means sooner or later you will also be doing it to yourself--because you cannot respect a thing long without doing it. It is getting to you, it is seeping into your heart.

Never respect anything unnatural! Respect nature, worship nature--but always remember that your respect and worship and love should be for nature, then it is for God. Otherwise it is all an ego game.

But that's how the mind functions. If you hear somebody lives only on water, you start getting excited. People go on moving to these unnatural, artificial, perverted people. It is very rare to find a natural saint, because if he is natural nobody will believe that he is a saint. To be a saint he finds to be unnatural.

One Christian saint remained thirty-seven years sitting on a pillar thirty feet high. He was worshipped all over the world. People used to come from thousands of miles just to pay respect to him. And he was simply sitting there, somehow managing, for thirty-seven years. He died there. If he was an ordinary simple man, do you think anybody would have taken the trouble to go and respect him? For what?

Mind is so much interested in perversion. Christians can't believe that Jesus was born normally; he has to be born out of a virgin mother, then it is special. Then it is against nature!--but then it is extraordinary. Buddha was not born out of a virgin mother, so he becomes ordinary, Christ becomes special. Buddhist have their stories to make their Buddha special: he was born while his mother was standing. And immediately when he dropped out of the womb, popped out of the womb, he walked--seven steps! He has to walk, otherwise he will be a natural ordinary child. Seven steps he walked and declared: "There is nobody higher than me, there has never been anybody higher than me."

Now, these foolish stories have to be invented because of your perverted mind. Then you seem attracted. You will not respect

Jesus if he simply goes in a boat on Lake Galilee. You will not respect him, you will say, "So what? Everybody does that." But he walks on the water--then there is something special. But just see the point: anything unnatural seems a miracle to you.

And what Ikkyu is saying and what I am insisting again and again is: the greatest miracle in this life and on this earth is to relax into nature--the greatest miracle, because that is the hardest thing for the ego to do.

You would also like to walk on water, wouldn't you? If I start teaching just now how to walk on water, all the people who have fallen asleep will be immediately awake. Then they will not miss. Who cares about enlightenment?--you can go on sleeping and there is always tomorrow. But walking on water? Then immediately you will bring yourself to awareness. You will say, "This is not to be missed, it happens only once in a while."

Just see how you are interested in the unnatural--you call it miraculous. There are no miracles, they have never happened, they don't happen, they can't happen. Because the law of nature is absolute: no exceptions are possible. Don't be befooled and deceived by the stories.

But one miracle is possible, and that is not against the law of nature. But it is miraculous because it rarely happens--that's why it is miraculous. You can fall in tune with nature. Immediately you become that which you are. And suddenly all misery and all hell disappears, all nightmares disappear, you are fully awake. And life takes a new colour, a new flavour. That flavour is divine, but it comes out of the natural law.

For my sannyasins, this is my message: Live naturally, as naturally as possible. Avoid the attraction towards the unnatural. The desire to be special, somebody in particular, is pathological. If you want to be special you will have to go against nature. And to go against nature is to go against God, because God is nature.

George Gurdjieff used to say that all the mahatmas are against God. And I agree with him, in toto--because they all teach you to

go against nature, they condemn nature. Everything that is natural
is immediately condemned. They have made God just absolutely
opposite to nature.

God is not opposite to nature, nature has arisen out of God.
Nature is a wave of God, and it will disappear into God again. It is
not against, it cannot be against God.

People come to me and they ask, "What kind of sannyasins are
you creating who don't renounce life?" I say: They renounce
unnatural ways of life. They don't renounce life--why should they?
God has not renounced life, otherwise he would have stopped the
whole business. He still goes on creating people; he still goes on
creating new flowers, new trees, new animals, new birds, new
planets--he is not tired. He has not bothered what your so-called
religious people say, he doesn't care at all. If he had listened to your
mahatmas he would have stopped creating the world--because
what is the point? He creates the world and then the mahatmas
persuade people to renounce it! He goes on creating, because he is
life; he can't help it. It is not that he is creating; he is creativity--it is
arising out of him spontaneously, naturally. It will continue.

Life has not to be renounced. And the sannyas that taught
people to renounce life was against life, against God, against the
Law of Buddhas and the Law of Men. I teach you a new sannyas:
to love life, to live life, to be life. Renounce unnatural methods and
ways; be natural.

And just the opposite has been said to you up to now. They say,
"Renounce the natural and become unnatural." That's why if they are
against me, very much worried by me, it seems natural; their being
against me seems to be very logical. I am putting things absolutely
upside-down for them. I say, "Live life--that is true sannyas." They
say, "Renounce life." Now, their sannyas and my sannyas are not
synonymous at all--polar opposites, diametrically opposite.

In this country the priest has been very important for centuries,
very dominant. He still dominates; this country is still not out of the
grip of the priest. He is against me, he goes on creating trouble for

my work--because he knows if I succeed then the whole business of the priesthood is destroyed for ever. The priest is afraid, the politician is afraid.

You have been hearing again and again that I am trying to find a place to move to. But Delhi is very much against it--they don't want me to have a bigger place, bigger space; they go on creating new kinds of hindrances. And they can create them: legal, this and that--at least they can delay and they can postpone. Their whole effort is so that somehow the world should not know about me. The Australian TV was coming to film the ashram, they were stopped. The BBC people had come, they had filmed half, and now they have been stopped by the government and they cannot film. And people call this the greatest democracy in the world.

Journalists are being prevented from coming here--the world should not know what is happening here, people should not come here. But the reason is clear, obvious. The reason is: whatsoever they have been thinking is religion, I say is not religion. In fact, what they say is religion is exactly anti-religion.

I am teaching you a new religion, a new dispensation, new in the sense that the priests have not allowed you to see it up to now--old and the ancient most in another sense, because those who have awakened have always taught the same.

Remember these sutras of Ikkyu, they are of immense import. If you decide to be special then you will go against nature and you will create pathology in your consciousness and you will become perverted.

I have heard about Catholic nuns... Now, they have been forced into a kind of celibacy. Celibacy arises, it cannot be forced. It is a spontaneous phenomenon--if you have lived your life rightly, celibacy comes on its own. Just as when you are fourteen sex arrives on its own, if you have lived your life rightly, nearabout forty-two celibacy starts arriving on its own. These are natural phenomena. Celibacy has not to be taught, has not to be practised. It will be as foolish as if you teach a seven-year-old child to practise sex--it will be as foolish and stupid. There is no need to teach the child to practise sex, it will come in its own time--the spring will come.

But no spring lasts for ever. The spring that is brought by the age fourteen will disappear by the age forty-two; it disappears naturally if you have lived naturally. But if you have not lived naturally and you have been repressing your sex, then it can continue up to eighty-two. Then dying also you will be thinking of sex.

The last thought in most people's minds when they die is sex, nothing else. It has to be, because that is their most repressed thing. And when they are dying they cling to sex--sex is just the opposite of death. With sex, life starts; with death, life ends. So when they are dying, to avoid death they start thinking of sex.

It is very rare to find a man who dies without thinking of sex. This is perversion, universal perversion. Celibacy comes on its own--when the time is right, when you have lived your dreams, your illusions, and you have seen that they are illusory, one day suddenly you see something has disappeared from you. Then you are almost puzzled by its disappearance--because it was so important up to now. It was the center of your life, the pivot you were revolving around, and suddenly it is no more there. Celibacy comes, has not to be practised.

One has only to live naturally and trust, and everything comes in its time. Celibacy comes, meditation comes, God comes, in its own time. Everything comes--just as you are born and you will die, everything else also comes. But somewhere you go perverted and then natural things don't happen. Then you remain in a kind of hung-up state.

Celibacy was forced on Christian nuns. And what happened? Do you know the story of the middle ages? Then those nuns started having hallucinations: Jesus comes and fondles their breasts. Now, what nonsense--Jesus coming and fondling their breasts? This is perversion. Jesus comes and makes love to them in the night; not only that, nuns started creating false pregnancies. Just hot air--nothing. But their bellies would swell.

And the church became very much concerned--what to do? Now, these poor women, they have been forced into celibacy, now they are hallucinating. The natural desire has been crushed; now it is coming from the back door. Then it was prohibited--because this is not moral on the part of Jesus to fondle nuns' breasts, this doesn't look good. And to come in the night and make love--and he will make them pregnant! This is not good on Jesus' part. So it was prohibited.

Then nuns started thinking that the Devil comes now. Finally, if you cannot have anybody else's support, the Devil is always available. The Devil is such a nice guy, the last resort--when you cannot find refuge anywhere, you can find refuge in the Devil. Then the Devil started coming. And when the Devil comes he comes in his own ways. Jesus must have been coming in a mild way--blessed are the meek. When the Devil comes he comes with a fanfare. He has a forked penis--a devil is a devil.

Now, these hallucinations are ugly, unnatural. But remember, they are not created by the nuns, they are created by the people who forced these poor girls to become nuns. It was an unnatural imposition.

And why, down the ages, have religions tried to repress your sex? For a certain very basic reason--you will be surprised to know about it, it is one of their trade secrets. They have always been against sex. Why? Because if sex energy is repressed then it becomes easy for a person to become interested in God. If no other outlet is left then the whole imagination, the whole capacity to dream, becomes focussed on God.

Now, this is cheating, cheating on God. The person is not really interested in God--just there is no other interest left, so all his interest starts flowing towards God. He starts hallucinating, then visions of Jesus and Krishna arise. These visions are absolutely imaginary, and if you allow the person natural sex these visions will immediately disappear.

It is as if you fast for a few days: you will hallucinate about food.

And if you are not even allowed to hallucinate about food, then the hallucination will have to find something else as an object to focus upon. This is a trick.

If no love affair is allowed to a person he will start loving God-- what else to do? It is almost inevitable to love God then. So religions have been using this device--deceptive, hallucinatory: stop people's imagination about sex and then the imagination will find its own outlet. And leave only one outlet open God--and close all the doors.

It is as if all the doors are closed and only one window is left: you will have to go out that window. If you want to go out, if you feel suffocated, what will you do? You will have to go out that window. It may be arduous, it may be ugly, it may be dangerous-- you may fall, you may break your legs--but you will have to go through that window.

This is a very very cunning device: repress people's sex and they will automatically start thinking of God. But this is not the true God, it is just a sex-substitute.

The true God does not arise as a substitute. The true God arises when you have lived your illusions and you have finished them, when you have seen through and through and all the illusions have been dropped. In that non-illusionary state of consciousness, you see God. Then that God is not a projection of your mind.

I would like
To offer you something,
But in the Daruma Sect
We have nothing at all.

IKKYU SAYS: We cannot offer you anything special, we can only offer you the natural. But that is nothing to offer, because it is already with you--you have it.

I would like
To offer you something...

Out of his love and compassion he wants to offer you
something. I want to offer you something, but I also don't have
anything to offer. On the contrary, a real master has to take
everything away from you. Slowly slowly, but certainly, he takes
things away from you. He persuades you to drop all the garbage
that you carry. He leaves you utterly empty.

In that emptiness, God happens. But God cannot be given,
truth cannot be transferred. It is untransferrable.

I would like
To offer you something,
But in the Daruma Sect
We have nothing at all.

A beautiful statement: Nothing at all. Yes, that's what a real
master gives you--nothing. He takes everything away, leaves
nothing behind. Out of that nothing your nature starts flowing--
because everything that is there is hindering your nature having its
say. Everything is a hindrance to your nature song.

As Ikkyu does not think of his body
As if it were his body,
He lives in the same place,
Whether it is town or country.

And Ikkyu says: There is no need to go to a mountain
monastery, you can live in the marketplace. God is available
everywhere, because the law of nature is functioning everywhere.
And the people who go on changing one place for another place
are misguided from the very beginning--because the question is
not of changing places, the question is of changing consciousness.

If you think you are the body, then it seems relevant not to live in the marketplace--go and live in a Himalayan cave. But you are not your body. So by changing--moving the body from the marketplace to the Himalayan caves--nothing will change, you will remain the same. You cannot leave yourself anywhere, you will be going with you! You are your consciousness.

As Ikkyu does not think of his body
As if it were his body,
He lives in the same place...

He lives in the world. But because he is not the body and he is not confined in the body, he knows his infinity and immortality. He knows his unbornness, undyingness. He knows his absolute emptiness which cannot be destroyed or changed or modified. He knows his skylike nature--clouds come and go, but they don't leave any track behind on the sky. The sky remains untouched, unmoved.

He lives in the same place.
Whether it is town or country.

Then it makes no difference; you can live wherever you are. Once you have relaxed into nature, once you have relaxed into your natural consciousness, once you are no more trying to be somebody special, you can live anywhere you are--because all is one law, the Law of Men and the Law of Buddha. In that very Law you have reached, you have entered the shrine of God.

The mind of man is without sound,
Without odour;
He who answers when called
Is nothing but a thief.

YOUR INNER CONSCIOUSNESS HAS NO SMELL, no taste,

no sound. It is untouchable, it is invisible. Become aware of it. And to be natural is the best way to be aware of it--because in being natural you relax, and when you relax you can see who you are. When you are tense and striving after something, you can't relax and you cannot see who you are. Your interest is more in who you would like to be--you are focussed on that. And because of that focussing you go on missing that which you already are.

When you are not trying to become anybody, when A is not trying to become B, how long can he avoid seeing that "I am A"? If A is trying to become B, he can go on avoiding seeing that "I am A." And A can never become B it is impossible. A is A, B is B.

In relaxing into nature one becomes aware of one's being.

The mind of man is without sound,
Without odour;
He who answers when called
Is nothing but a thief.

And then, when you know "Who am I?" don't think that you will be able to answer the question. If somebody asks you, "Who are you?" don't think that you will be able to answer it.

The emperor Wu of China asked Bodhidharma, "Who are you?" And Bodhidharma said, "I don't know, Sir." And he was the man who knew; he was amongst those few men who know. But he said, "I don't know."

Wu could not understand him, You would also have missed. You would also have thought that if he knows, then he should say. "Who am I?" If you go to a traditional swami, a sannyasin, a mahatma, and you ask, "Who are you?" he will say, "*Shivohum*! I am God. *Aham Brahmasmi*! I am the absolute, I am the suprememost soul"--and all that nonsense. Bodhidharma said, "I don't know."

Ikkyu is saying:

He who answers when called
Is nothing but a thief.

These people who say *Aham Brahmasmi* are just thieves--they
have borrowed words from others. One who knows, cannot say.
He will look into your eyes with all his emptiness pouring through
his eyes...he may hold your hand, he may sit in silence with you.
But he cannot answer that question, "Who are you?" If you insist,
he will say, "I don't know"--because it is so vast, it cannot become
part of knowledge. And it is known only when all words disappear--
so to use words for it is to be a thief. Those words are relevant in
the world, they are not relevant in that consciousness. It is stealing
words from the world, from this, to explain that. And that is not
possible.

If we say " There is,"
People think " There is";
But though it answers,
It is not,
This mountain echo.

The problem is, Ikkyu says, if we say "There is somebody in
me"--a self, a god, or something...

If we say "There is,"
People think "There is";
But though it answers,
It is not,
This mountain echo.

Whatsoever is said is just a mountain echo; it is not the true
thing. It is echoed in words--silence echoed in words,
soundlessness echoed in words: it is an echo, a mountain echo.
Remember this phrase: This mountain echo.

But people start believing in it. And that is the danger of saying, "I am the supreme self." Then they start believing that they are supreme selves; then belief is created. And around belief priests arise, temples are built. Around belief churches are created, and around belief politics arises.

If we say, " There is not,"
People think "There is not,"
Though it answers,
The mountain echo.

If we say "It is," people start believing it is. If we say "It is not," people start believing it is not. Both are untrue--because the truth is such, there is no way to say it, either through the positive or through the negative. All words falsify it, belie it.

And these are the two kinds of people in the world. In Russia they believe it is not, in China now they believe it is not. In India, in America, in Germany, they believe it is. But how do you believe? If you observe deeply you will not find any difference between an Indian and a Russian. The Russian is being told "There is no God" so he repeats "There is no God." The Indian is told "There is God" so he repeats "There is God." Do you think there is any difference? On the surface there seems to be a great difference-- one is an atheist, another is a theist; one believes, one disbelieves. But do you think there is really a difference? Both have been told something, and both have believed it.

Before 1917, before the revolution in Russia, people were as religious as they are in India. In fact, Russia was one of the most religious countries in the world. Then what happened? Within ten years' time, all that religion, that centuries-old religion, disappeared like vapour--as if it had never been there.

What happened? The people in power started saying "God is not." And the masses only repeat, the masses only follow blindly. Religion disappeared within ten years. The work of centuries, maybe ten thousand years' work, disappeared in ten years! What kind of religion is this?

And this happened again in China. China is one of the ancientmost countries, maybe the most ancient: has the ancientmost scriptures, the longest tradition: of religion-- Confucianism, Taoism, Buddhism--has created great enlightened people, has always lived in a religious way. And what happened? Suddenly all the Bibles, Korans, Dhammapadas, Vedas, Tao Te Ching, Analects of Confucius--all disappeared. And people started carrying a small red book written by Mao Tse Tung; that became their Bible. Suddenly God no more exists, the soul is just nonsense, meditation a wastage of time; prayer, foolishness. Temples toppled down, monasteries evaporated: within a few years, all was gone.

And do you think if communism comes to India, things will be different? Not at all. I see into people's eyes--their religion is as bogus as it was in Russia, as it was in China. If the people who are in authority and power start saying there is no God and they start shouting on the TV and the radio, "There is no God!" people will start repeating that. People have always been repeating.

Ikkyu is right, he says:

If we say " There is,"
People think "There is";
But though it answers,
It is not,
This mountain echo.

Although we have said "It is," this is just an echo. Don't believe in an echo; an echo is an echo. You will have to go yourself to see what the case is.

If we say, "There is not,"
People think "There is not,"

Though it answers,
The mountain echo.

That's what you are, believers in mountain echoes--that's what
your religion consists of. You are deceiving yourself. Drop all these
deceptions. There is no way to believe anybody, whosoever he is--
Christ or Buddha or me. There is no way to believe in anybody.
The only way towards God is through experiencing, not through
believing. Believing, you will miss.

Drop beliefs--this way or that, for or against. And remember, the
person who says "I don't believe in God" is not really the person I
mean. He believes that there is no God: that is his belief. The
communist believes that there is no God--not that he does not
believe.

A real person has no belief, for or against. He cannot say God
is, he cannot say God is not. How can you say without knowing
"God is not"? And how can you say without knowing "God is"?
Both are stupid statements. You can only say "I don't know"--that
will be authentic, true, honest. And you can start only from there: "I
don't know."

And see the beauty of it. One starts by saying "I don't know"
because one really does not know. Then one starts moving deeper
and deeper, and one day one comes to know. And then Emperor
Wu asks Bodhidharma, "Who are you?" and Bodhidharma says,
"Sir, I don't know."

It begins in "I don't know," it ends in "I don't know", but with a
great difference. In the beginning when you say "I don't know" it is
just a statement of a fact, that you don't know, how can you say
yes or no? But when you end and you say "I don't know" it is a
statement of truth, not of fact. You have known--but whatsoever
has been known is so vast, no word can contain it. Only your being
can say it, your presence can say it.

Reading sutras like Ikkyu's, or reading the words of
Bodhidharma, or listening to me, always remember that we are

using the same words as you use but the meaning is different. For that, one has to be very alert, otherwise misunderstanding arises.

I have heard:

It was an international television conference in the USA and the delegates were eating the farewell dinner of the conference.

A Japanese gentleman was sitting next to a delegate from Portland, Oregon. After the Japanese had finished his soup, the American asked him, "Likee soupee?" The Japanese gentleman nodded.

Throughout the meal, the American asked such questions as: "Likee fishee?" and "Likee drinkee?"

When the meal was finished, the chairman of the conference rose to his feet and introduced the Japanese gentleman as the guest speaker of the meeting.

The Oriental gentleman gave a witty, excellent speech on the future of broadcasting--speaking in English much better than anything any American has ever uttered.

After his speech, the Japanese gentleman returned to his seat and asked his American table companion: "Likee speechee?"

Communication is a problem, a great problem.

These people like Ikkyu speak the same language and yet they don't speak the same language. You will have to be very patient, very loving, open and sympathetic to understand. Only then will these sutras reveal their significance into your being. These sutras can open the door which has never been closed.

THE FLIGHT
OF THE ALONE TO
THE ALONE

It all seems so simple--
I just can't understand it!

Who is more stupid--
man or woman?

What is the difference between
learning and collecting knowledge?

Why am I so afraid of you?

The first question

It all seems so simple--I just can't understand it. I keep grasping at it and it eludes me, a music that can almost be smelt, a taste that can almost be felt. Sometimes I am on the very threshold; other times it's not in a million years, not for me.

KRISHNA PRABHU, IT IS SIMPLE, hence it is impossible to understand it. If it was complex, understanding would be possible. Only a complex thing can be understood, because a complex thing can be analyzed, divided, broken into parts. A simple thing is indivisible; you cannot analyze it, you cannot dissect it. It is simply there; it is impossible to understand it.

That's why all that is simple eludes knowledge. God is simple, that's why science cannot know him. Love is simple, that's why science can have no idea what it is. Whenever you come across a simple thing you have to drop the effort to understand it; only then can you understand it. A totally new kind of understanding will be needed--an understanding of the heart, which does not analyze, which does not dissect.

See: science dissects, analyzes, divides. It goes on trying to find the smaller and the smaller part--it reaches to the atom, to the electron, and it goes on dividing. It will never know about the whole, it will know only about the parts. And once it comes against a part which cannot be divided, again it is elusive.

Now, science knows nothing about the electrons yet, because they can't be divided yet. Once you divide them you will know--you will know how they are composed, of what they are composed. But then again you are facing something else--the new division--and that eludes knowledge.

Religion moves in a totally different way. It does not go to the part, it goes to the whole. 'God' means the whole--the undivided whole, the totality of all. How can you understand God? In the very effort to understand, you have become separate from it; God is no more total. The one who is trying to understand is separate--division has started, you are on the way to science. The known and the knower have become separate; the first division has happened. Now it is a process ad infinitum.

God can be known only if you remain in an undivided relatedness with the whole. You don't become a knower, you don't become an observer. You don't stand out of it--you can't. You are in it, you are it--how can you know it? You can be it! And that is a totally different kind of knowing, a different kind of understanding-- the understanding that arises out of being.

You cannot know love from the outside, but you can be love-- and then you will know. But that knowing will not be part of your head. The head will still remain ignorant; you will know, but you will not be able to translate it into the language that the head can understand.

You ask me: It all seems so simple...

Not that it seems simple, it is simple! But you have been taught again and again that if something is simple you will be able to understand it immediately. That is absolute nonsense. The simple is impossible to understand. The simple is elusive; there is no meeting between the effort to understand and between that which is simple. Either the simple has to be denied...If you say that it doesn't exist then you are okay, then the problem has been dropped.

That's what science has been doing: "There is no God, there is no soul, there is no love." Deny all those simple things, then you can at least have your peace of mind; there is nothing left which haunts you. Science denies God just in self-defence--otherwise God stands there like an impossible problem. And the scientist cannot become a knower if even God has not been understood. And God cannot be understood. The simple way is: say that there is no God, so there is no question of understanding. Then you are at ease.

Religion says: God is, only God is. In fact to say 'God is' is repetitive, because God means *is-ness*. All that is, is God; God is not a separate entity. This *is-ness*, just this, is God. How can you understand it? You have to drop understanding, you have to become ignorant. If you approach God with your knowledge, knowledgeability, you will go on missing. You have to drop all your knowledge. You have to allow your scriptures to disappear, your doctrines to depart; say goodbye to them, and for ever.

And suddenly, the moment you are in a state of no-knowledge, that is the state of meditation--the state of no-knowledge, the state of innocence.

Blessed are the ignorant. Why? Because only they can know. Jesus goes on saying to his disciples, "Unless you are like small children you will not enter into my kingdom of God." Why small children? Innocent, ignorant, non-knowledgeable. Carrying nothing in the mind, just empty, with no ideas, no thoughts to project--not in any way trying to understand.

Innocence gives you wonder, creates awe. You simply feel a great Aha! like a tidal wave arising in your being. Body, mind, soul, all are involved in this Aha! All has stopped. You are there--not as a knower, you are dissolved as a knower. And then the knowing happens, because then the being happens. Then you are in tune with the whole.

That harmony, that rhythm, that togetherness with the whole, is what religion calls understanding. You are not to be an observer-- in fact you are not to be at all. Then the simple is understood. And the simple is great, and the simple has splendour.

You say: It all seems so simple--I just can't understand it.

True. You can't, nobody can. Drop the effort--that effort will tire you. And when one becomes too tired doing something impossible, one starts denying it. If you cannot know, you cannot know, you cannot know...a moment comes when it is too much to tolerate it. The question becomes heavy on your heart. For sheer self-defence you start saying, "It is not there. If it was there then I would have understood it. Because I cannot understand it, it cannot be there. It is. pseudo-puzzle. God is not there--a created problem."

Then you can rest. You can go back to sleep, you can walk again, you can again live your mediocre life. It is the cowards who deny God--cowards because they cannot gather courage to be ignorant enough to know the simple.

I have heard:

The farmer had just returned from a drive in his carriage. His dog, who had been running alongside, threw himself on the grass, his sides heaving with his heavy panting. "It is not the road that tires him," explained the farmer, "but his zig-zagging. We have ridden for about five miles, but the dog has covered twenty-five miles. There was not a cat he did not chase, not a dog he did not bark at, not a driveway he did not investigate. Straight travelling did not tire him, only the zig-zagging did."

Philosophy is zig-zagging. Religion is straight.

Jesus says, "My way is straight and narrow." Religion is the shortest possible way between two points--between the knower and the known, the shortest possible way. It joins the knower and the known directly, without any zig-zagging. Philosophy zig-zags, and zig-zags so much that finally it loses all track of the goal.

What is the shortest distance between two points? Love is the shortest distance between two points--two alive points, two beings, two existences. Love is the shortest distance, knowledge the longest.

And that's why religion has a totally different dimension in relating to existence. Those who have become accustomed to zig-zagging--analyzing, interpreting, philosophizing--they will go on chasing every cat, every dog, they will go on exploring every driveway, and they will be tiring themselves and reaching nowhere. They don't have any sense of direction.

The simple man, the innocent man, simply goes straight.

And Jesus also says, "The way is straight and narrow." Why narrow? It is so narrow that it cannot contain your ego. Only you can go--but you will have to leave your ego outside, outside the door. It is so narrow, two persons cannot walk together. You cannot take your child with you, you cannot take your aging mother with you, you cannot take your beloved with you.

Even a Buddha cannot take you with him. Buddhas only point the way--because two persons cannot walk on it, it is so narrow. One has to go alone: the flight of the alone to the alone. And so alone that not even your ego is with you, and so alone that not even your mind is with you, and so utterly alone that not even your self is with you.

You go into it as absolute silence, as a disappearing person, as an appearing presence.

It all seems so simple--I just can't understand it. I keep grasping at it and it eludes me...

That's why it eludes you. Not that it is elusive; that is not its nature. It appears to elude you, Krishna Prabhu, because you are trying to grasp it. You create the elusiveness in it by your grasping.

There are things which cannot be grasped. You cannot grasp the sky in your hand--or can you? You cannot grasp it in your fist; if you try you will miss. The more the fist becomes strong, closed, the less sky it will have in it. Open the fist and you have the whole sky available.

But mind is very much a miser, a hoarder. It always hoards; it immediately closes up on things. If you know something you immediately close up on it, you immediately reduce it to knowledge. That's why knowing is constantly being reduced to knowledge--and the moment you reduce knowing to knowledge you have killed it. Then you have only a dead bird in your hands--it cannot fly into the sky; then you will never see it again on its wings.

Knowing is alive, a bird on the wing. Knowledge is a killed bird--it is in your hands, but you can only have the dead body. The soul has flown, and that was the real thing, the essential thing. You have missed the real and you are hoarding the unreal. But that's our way, that's what we do with everything. Knowing is immediately reduced to knowledge.

Leave your knowing as knowing! Existence consists not of nouns but of verbs. All nouns are false: no noun is true, can be true. There is no tree, there are only treeing phenomena. There is no river, only riverings.

When you say, "This is a man," what are you saying? You are reducing a verb to a noun--because the man is growing! It is a growth, it is a process. It is not the same even for two seconds, it is a flow. You say, "This is my friend"--but the time that you take in saying "This is my friend" may be enough to turn him into your enemy.

You say 'love'? There is no love, only loving. See life and you will be surprised: there is no life, only living.

Reduce all nouns to verbs and you will have a far clearer perspective of life. But no verb can be grasped. Nouns can be grasped; because of the miserly mind, man lives through nouns and has forgotten verbs.

And this miserliness penetrates into everything you do. Why grasp? You see a beautiful flower and immediately you are on the way to pluck it. Why? It was beautiful on the stem, alive, rooted in God. And you killed it. And are you thinking you are going to give it to your girlfriend? You are presenting death to your girlfriend! Or do you think you are going to put this flower at the feet of the god in the temple? That god is dead, this flower is dead, and between these two deaths you are dead. The flower was already offered to God on the bush--it was with God, you took it away from God to offer it to a stone. Why this immediate desire to pluck the flower?

I have heard: A friend was visiting George Bernard Shaw. He was very much against people plucking flowers from his garden-- he had put notice-boards all over the garden: "Don't Pluck Flowers." The friend asked, "Don't you love flowers? Don't you like flowers being arranged on your table?"

Bernard Shaw said, "I love flowers, that's why. I love children too, but I would not like anybody to cut off their heads and arrange those heads on my table."

The idea of the ego is always to kill and destroy. Why? Because once a thing is destroyed you are in control. You can control only dead things. That's why people worship dead gods in the temples, and they worship dead masters.

When Buddha is alive they will not worship him, they will worship Krishna. When Buddha is gone they will worship Buddha, they will not worship Christ. When Christ is gone they will worship Christ, they will not worship Kabir--and so on and so forth. Once a master is gone, great shrines are raised in his name and people start worshipping him. But while he is alive they stone him to death, they crucify him, they reject him, they deny him. Why? Why are you so much interested in death?

With death you become masters. With an alive master you cannot be in control, he will be in control. With an alive flower the flower is in control, not you; once plucked, you are in control. Then you can go on doing any stupid nonsense--you can call it *ikebana* and you can go on arranging flowers and you can go on learning flower arrangement, and that is all nonsense.

You have destroyed the flower, now you are feeling guilty. Hence *ikebana*--it is out of guilt. Now you are trying somehow to pretend that you are creating beauty again. There is deep guilt-- you have destroyed beauty. It was perfectly beautiful on the bush, on the stem, in the wind, with the sun.

But the mind has a constant desire to grasp. Watch this miserliness. I have heard:

A rich old miser became critically ill and the doctor prescribed a medicine with the following warning: "If after taking the medicine you perspire, it is a sign that you will recover. If you don't perspire, only God can help."

The miser took the medicine, but failed to perspire. It seemed that the rich man was about to die.

"Let us call on him," said the mayor to the elders of the town. "Perhaps he will now repent his ways and leave something for the church."

They visited him, and found him in a repentant mood. They brought paper and ink and the mayor got ready to write. "The church," he said, "is badly in need of repairs."

"A hundred dollars for the church," said the miser, and groaned.

"The widows and orphans fund is depleted," said the mayor.

"A hundred...wait a minute, wait a minute!" the miser cried suddenly. "Cross it out! I'm perspiring! I'm perspiring!"

The mind is always clinging to things. It may be money, it may be meditation. It may be knowledge, it may be love. Watch that the mind always wants to grasp, hold things in hand.

Now, you cannot hold God in your hand. You can hold a flower, you can pluck a flower, but you cannot hold God in your hand. God is too big for that. God means totality. How can you hold this totality in your hand? One has to approach in a different way--one has to surrender oneself into God's hands. Rather than grasping God, you have to pray to be grasped by him.

You cannot hold the ocean in your hands, but you can drop into the ocean and disappear. That's the way to be it.

I keep grasping at it and it eludes me, a music that can almost be smelt, a taste that can almost be felt.

If you go on grasping that will remain so, and for ever. You will always be just on the verge, and missing. It will be a music that can almost be smelt--but an almost smelt music has not been heard at all. And almost is almost; it is just a way of deluding oneself. Either you have it or you don't have it--you can't say, "I almost have it." You are alive or you are not alive--you cannot say, "I am almost alive." You cannot say, "I am almost in love." Either this or that--it is either/or, and there is no middle way. You will always be on the threshold and missing.

Stop grasping at it, drop that very effort to grasp. Allow it to enter into you, be open to it, be vulnerable. Let him grasp you, let him possess you--don't try to possess him.

Sometimes I am on the very threshold; other times it's not in a million years, not for me.

And you will be on this see-saw. Again and again you will think you are on the threshold--just one step more and the bird will be in your hands. But that one step will remain impossible. And then of course you feel frustrated--how long can you remain in hope, just standing on the threshold? You become tired. When you become tired, it is a million years away from you...Again you start striving, again one day you will feel it is just on the threshold. This way it will remain--this is how seekers go on missing.

Seeking is not the way to find God. If you want to find him, stop seeking, and find. Stop seeking, and he is found immediately, instantly--not even a single moment is lost. Why? Because in the very effort of seeking him you are forgetting one thing, that he is already in you. The sought is in the seeker--but the seeker cannot see it, he is engrossed too much in his seeking. He is running after it, he is searching for it--his search keeps him so occupied, so engaged, that he cannot look inside and see who is there.

God is already in you, God is already the case. Just stop seeking. And that is the greatest message of Zen: Stop seeking. "Sitting silently, doing nothing, the spring comes and the grass grows by itself." Zen does not give you any seeking, it takes all seeking away from you. Seekers are the losers! because in their very search they go on looking at distant lands. They go on looking at stars--they don't look within themselves.

And do you know? There is an ancient parable:

In the beginning when God created the world, he used to live on MG Road. But then he became tired, because people were continuously nagging him. In the middle of the night the phone would start ringing, and complaints....

"Why have you not done this?" and "Why have you done this, and what is the reason for it?" Naturally he got tired.

He asked his counsellors, "Help me. I would like to go somewhere and hide from people." He confessed, "In creating man I have committed my greatest mistake." Do you know? since then he has not created anything else; he is still repenting. That was his last--he became so afraid of man that he stopped being a creator.

They suggested, "You can go to the Himalayas, nobody will come there." And he said, "You don't know, within just a few seconds"...and millions of light years are just a few seconds for God--a different time scale. For one who lives in eternity, millions of light years are just moments. He said, "Within moments, you don't know, a man will be there--Hillary. And Tensing will be there, and they will reach Everest and find me. And once they have found me then the whole MG Road--then people will start moving there. That won't help."

Somebody suggested, "Then why don't you go to the moon?" He said, "Just a few seconds more, and people will reach there. They are going to reach everywhere!"

Then an old adviser came close to him and whispered something in his ear. And he was very happy and he said "This is the right thing to do." The mall had whispered in his ear, "My suggestion is: why don't you hide in man himself? There he will never go. He will go to the mountains, he will go to Everest, he will go to the moon and to Mars and he will go to the planets and stars--he will go everywhere. One thing he will never suspect is that you can be hiding within his own soul."

God agreed. And since then he has been hiding in you, And you have been searching for him on Everest, on the moon, on the stars, in the scriptures, in the temples, in the mosques, in the churches...Go on searching and you will not find him.

A seeker never finds. Seeking is a sure way of missing. Then who finds him? One who relaxes, one who drops all seeking--just dives deep into one's own being, sits there silently, starts moving towards the bottom, to the very ground of one's own being. Sitting in your deepest core, you find him. There is no need to go anywhere.

If you are a seeker, and Krishna Prabhu seems to be a seeker...

Sometimes I am on the very threshold...

Yes, it will happen again and again. Again and again you will think, "Now! This time I am going to make it, it is going to happen." And it will never happen. Then again frustration and the dark night of the soul will follow. Many times you will see that you have almost made it, ninety-nine percent made it--but it will never be a hundred percent. And unless it is a hundred percent it is not at all. 'Almost' means nothing, 'approximately' means nothing. That one step is as far away as millions of light years, because it cannot be taken.

So after each euphoria, elation, ecstasy, after each feeling of "Now I have arrived," there will be great depression. You will fall back into a dark hole. Again you will have to grope, again you will have to reach that threshold, and again you will fall.

This has been continuing for so many lives--you are not new here. You have been playing this game for millions of lives: coming closer, coming closer, coming closer, and you feel the ecstasy, now you are just there...and all is missed again, you are falling far away, far away, again disappearing. This wheel goes on moving.

You have to jump out of this wheel. He is not out, so you can never come close to him. If he was far away from you then there would be a possibility sometimes to come close, and there would be a possibility to cross the threshold and reach him and hold him. He is not out, he is your innermost core. He is the beat of your heart and the vitality of your breath and the redness of your blood. He is the pulsation of your being. How can you be just on the threshold?

You have to forget all these thresholds and you have to forget all these distances. And remember always: to be close is also to be distant. Closeness is a kind of distance; you are not yet it.

I teach you the way of non-seeking. I teach you to relax. I teach you to forget all about God and just be yourself.

And one day suddenly, like a great surprise, comes the benediction.

The second question

Who is more stupid--man or woman?

PREM PUNEETA, I have heard an anecdote:

A man was saying to his woman, "Why has God made you women so beautiful?" The woman said, "So that you men can fall in love with us."
The man then said, "Then why did he make you so stupid?" And the woman said, "So that we can also fall in love with you."
But in reality, stupidity has no sex. It is found in all kinds and all shapes and all sizes.

The third question

What is the difference between learning and collecting knowledge?

GREAT DIFFERENCE IS THERE. They are polar opposites, diametrically opposite to each other.
Learning is never knowledge, learning is knowing. Knowledge is never learning, it is a pretension of learning. knowledge is pseudo, borrowed. You become a parrot, you become an imitator. You become a computer, you function as a memory machine--you don't know exactly what you think you know, you simply repeat it. And you can become very clever in repeating, very skillful, but s ill you remain a parrot.
Learning is to encounter truth on your own. Knowledge is borrowed, knowledge is from others.
If you listen to Ikkyu and you learn his beautiful sutras--and you can learn them by heart and you can repeat them; not only repeat them, you can even try to follow them--you can create a character according to them. You can live them too, but still it is borrowed. Not only will your knowledge be false and plastic, your character will also be plastic and borrowed, enforced.
Deep down you will remain the same; nothing will have

changed. You will have become richer as far as information is concerned, but you will not be transformed by it. No information ever transforms anybody.

Knowledge is the collection and accumulation of information. Learning is the availability to be transformed. Knowledge always goes to dead masters, learning is always in search of living masters--because you can learn only through a living phenomenon. There is no way to learn from a dead phenomenon; it is cheap.

A disciple with a Zen master has to pass through a thousand and one pains. And you simply read the whole story within minutes, but it took him thirty years to become enlightened. And those thirty years of agony and ecstasy, those thirty years of falling in love with the master and hating him from the very guts--of moving closer to him and going far away from him, of falling into his being, and yet fighting with him--those thirty years of constant meditation and love, of great effort, and finally of knowing the futility of all effort; of great seeking and search, and finally coming to realize that no seeking is needed--but one comes to it the hard way.

Then one day those thirty years of ripening and maturity bring an integration. One blooms. The satori happens. One understands, one sees.

You simply read it on one page of a book, and this becomes knowledge to you. And sometimes you can say things....

Once it happened, a young man lived with me for three years, and he was in deep love with the Zen approach. And whenever he would see a story--and there are thousands--where the master hits the disciple on the face or strikes him with his stick, the young man would bring the story to me and he would say, "How cute!"

One day I slapped him hard. And he was angry, and he forgot all those stories. And he said, "Are you mad or something? Why did you hit me? And I had not done anything!"

And I asked him, "Now say 'How cute!'"

Then it doesn't look cute. Knowledge is cheap, you don't pay anything for it. Learning is hard, arduous; you have to pay for it. Inch by inch, you have to die into it. Knowledge is accumulation, learning is not really accumulation at all--on the contrary, it is just a reverse process.

The master goes on taking things away from you. He does not give you something to be added to your personality, he takes all the props of your personality. And one day suddenly you find yourself collapsing...

One can allow that collapse only if there has arisen a great trust. And when you have collapsed, then like a phoenix the new being arrives. Remember always, the new being is not any change in the old being. The new being is absolutely new, it is not a change in the old being. The old is dead and the new has arrived; they are discontinuous.

The real change only happens through death. Unless death has happened you will only be accumulating, decorating, giving finishing touches to your personality. Yes, you will change little bits here and there, but that will be nothing much. Changing paintings from one wall to another, or painting the walls with a new colour, renovating the ruins, changing the carpet or arranging the furniture in a new style...But basically, fundamentally, you remain the same. These changes are not learning.

A learner is one who is ready to die. If you are after knowledge you are a student. If you are a learner you are a disciple. And it is so easy to be a student, it is so difficult to be a disciple. One goes on missing...

Just the other night, it happened. A beautiful woman came just a few days before, and started feeling a great urge to become a sannyasin, the urge to become a disciple. Then she was coming to take sannyas but could not enter because of her body smell or something. Next day she changed her mind. She said, "I am happy that I could not enter, otherwise I would have become a sannyasin. And I cannot wear orange clothes all the time in my work; it will look so weird, ridiculous, people will laugh."

Now you cannot pay even that much. It is not much! People laugh at you even without your orange clothes--don't be worried about that; they laugh all the same. Just as you laugh at them, they laugh at you. That's how people manage to laugh a little bit-- otherwise life is so bad, such an agony, a nightmare, if they don't laugh at each other they will commit suicide. It helps; just laughing at each other they feel unburdened. Seeing the ridiculousness of life, they can manage to laugh a little bit. It gives them heart to live again tomorrow.

Man can live without the Bible and without the Gita, but man cannot live without jokes--those small jokes are far more important. And have you ever noticed the fact that the Jews have the best jokes in the world? Why? Because they have suffered the most. They had to create jokes, otherwise they would have committed suicide long before. Those jokes have kept them alive. They have been tortured, down the ages; they have lived against odds. What has helped them to go on living? Do you think it is the Old Testament? Do you think it is the Talmud?

No. It is their capacity to laugh. It is their capacity to continue having a sense of humour that has kept them alive. That's why they have the best jokes in the world.

Hindus don't have jokes. They have lived a very very convenient life--jokes were not needed; life was comfortable, convenient. When life is too much to bear, one has to create something or other to have a little laughter to unburden oneself.

People are already laughing at you--they have to laugh. it is their survival; they cannot survive without it. So don't feel offended when people laugh at you, not at all. They are not really laughing at you, they are simply finding any excuse to laugh--you are as good as anybody else. If you are not in orange they will find something else. And I don't think you are so perfect that they cannot find anything else about you to laugh at.

But just a small price, that they will laugh, and one can drop the idea of becoming a sannyasin.

Just see how cheap we want transformation. We want it to be handed to us, bottle-fed. We want it to just be given to us, injected--digested by somebody else. Then it becomes knowledge. Buddha has said something, Krishna has said something, Christ has said something--you can just learn those words, you can become a chatterbox. And it doesn't matter what that chatter is--worldly or other-worldly, it is chatter all the same. Because you have not experienced anything on your own.

The first honesty for a man who really wants to know truth is to know perfectly well "what I know on my own", and "what I know only as borrowed." And whatsoever is borrowed, throw it! It is all crap. It is better to be ignorant on your own--because that is true, authentic, sincere--than to be knowledgeable on somebody else's experience. And who knows whether that experience was true or not? Who knows?--that man may himself have been repeating others' experiences.

Unless you know by yourself, there is no way.

You ask me: What is the difference between learning and collecting knowledge?

Prem Nath, the difference is great, as great as it can be. Learning needs courage, learning needs a transformation in your consciousness--a death and a resurrection. Knowledge needs nothing, just a little capacity to memorize--and any mediocre person can do that. Knowledge needs no intelligence, only memory. Learning needs intelligence.

And these are two different things. Intelligence is a quality of your soul, and memory is just a brain mechanism. Memory is just a bio-computer--the computer can do it far better than your bio-computer has been doing up to now. Sooner or later, people will be carrying small computers in their pockets rather than reading books, going to the university--that is really all out of date now. There is no future for schools and universities; the computer will destroy them all.

What is the point of knowing history? You can have a small computer in your pocket and you can inquire whenever there is a need; you can just inquire of the computer.

You can ask when Napoleon the Great was born, what date, what day, with which women he fell in love--you can inquire about everything. A computer can carry millions of pieces of information in just a small box. All the information that you are carrying, a computer can carry better. What is the need? This is a very, very bullock-cart way--twenty-five years studying in a college, school, university. And what is really being done there? You are being fed with knowledge; your bio-computer is being trained.

Sooner or later, you will be able to purchase a ready-made, trained bio-computer and it will answer! That day is going to be a great revolutionary day in human history, because from that day it will be simple to know what the difference is between learning and knowledge. A man who carries a computer is a man of knowledge, and a man who has his own experience of life is a wise man.

And remember, a computer can give you information but cannot give you experience. You can ask the computer: "What is love?" and the computer can report all that has been said about love. But that will not give you the experience of love; experience you can only have on your own. You will have to fall in love and know it--no computer can give it to you.

The computer can give all the information about God, but to know about God is not to know God. To know God is totally different. It is an encounter: it is personal, intimate, immediate.

And you can see it. The knowledgeable man almost always behaves stupidly. He has to behave so, because his knowledge is borrowed; he cannot behave intelligently. Pundits are the most stupid people in the world.

Two men were walking. One was holding a closed umbrella--he was a great pundit, a professor of philosophy. Suddenly it began to rain. "Open your umbrella, quickly," said one man to the other.

"It won't help at all," came the answer.

"What do you mean, it won't help? It will protect us from the rain."

"It is no use, the umbrella is full of holes like a sieve."

"Then why did you take it in the first place?

And the professor said, "Because I didn't think it was going to rain."

The man who carries information is just doing things like that. He does not know how to use it, he does not know why he is carrying it in the first place. He does not know anything. He has been given the information by his parents, by the teachers and priests, and he has been carrying it without even becoming aware why he is carrying it all.

Just look in your head, how many things you are carrying. For what? Those problems don't exist any more, and you are carrying the solutions of those problems. You have become mature, and still you are carrying the advice your mother gave to you when you were a child. Now you are no more a child, you can forget all about it--and it will be good, it will create a space in your head. Otherwise it has become a junkyard.

Just listen sometimes, silently sitting--still your mother's voice is heard. Your father says things to you and you still have to follow them, and if you don't follow them you feel guilty! because you are betraying your father. And the father, the poor father, is dead and he does not know anything of what he has done to the son. In fact he has not done anything; his father has done it to him, he has done it to you, and so on and so forth.

Many times sannyasins come to me, particularly women, and they say, "We want to have children." And all that I see...They think that they are asking for children because they are in such a great loving space. Not at all--when I look into them, all that I see is that they are wanting to have revenge on their mothers. Whatsoever their mothers have done to them, now they want children so they can do it to them. Otherwise how will they get rid of it?

Children are so dependent on you, you can do anything to them. They cannot retaliate, they cannot say no. And you are hankering, full of knowledge that your mother has given to you--your head is heavy with it, and you want somebody into whom you can pour all that nonsense. And you will feel very relieved; women feel very relieved when they have children.

What relief comes? It is a catharsis, a vomit. It is very rarely that out of love you think of a child, because you don't know what love is. How can you think out of love? You have never loved! But all that you need is a helpless dependent child who will always look up to you, and you will always be the boss and you can mould and pummel and manufacture the child to your heart's desire. That is the only way you can take revenge on your mother; there is no other way.

I have heard a story; it happened in the court of the great Akbar. He had a very wise man, Birbal, with him. They were standing and talking about something, and Birbal said something and Akbar became so angry that he hit him hard on the face, slapped him, before the court. Birbal was red with rage, but to hit back would be too costly. But if you don't do anything, that looks too humiliating. So he hit somebody else who was standing by his side--he hit him back.

And the man said, "But why are you hitting me?"

Birbal said, "Hand it on to somebody else."

That's how things happen. Now, your mother has hit you hard--you are still crying. You want to hit somebody, you want to hand it all over; you will be relieved.

Your parents are still alive in you. Your teachers, primary-school teachers--who knew nothing much, otherwise why should they have been primary-school teachers?--they are still alive and dominating you. Your college professors, they knew nothing, they were as borrowed as you are.

It is very rare to find a man who knows himself. Just imitators are all around, and you are still carrying their wisdom that they have given to you. They never lived their wisdom, and you are trying to live it; you also cannot live it. When you cannot live it you fool guilty, if you live it you feel unnatural; you are in a predicament.

This is the predicament every human being is in. If you follow whatsoever has been told to you to do, it is unnatural; it never makes you happy, it never gives you joy. Only one thing is good about it, it never makes you feel guilty--but it makes you sad, it makes you depressed. If you don't follow it then you feel guilty-- that too brings a kind of sadness.

Have you not watched it in your life? It is so difficult to be happy--why? Because happiness and guilt have become associated in you. So whenever you feel happy you feel something wrong must be there, you must be doing something wrong. Look inside yourself! into your files, and you will immediately come across a parental voice: "Don't do this." That's why you are feeling guilty. Happiness has never been allowed to you in your childhood. You don't allow it to yourself either.

My whole work here consists of this thing: to help you to allow happiness to yourself, to prepare you so that you can give the gift of happiness to yourself. God has given it to you, but your parents have disturbed it.

And don't feel angry at them--because they were also victims of their parents. It is a vicious circle; it is a very very long circle, it has been going on down the ages. Don't feel angry, but get rid of them! Drop their voices. Start living your life.

A man of knowledge never lives his own life. A man of learning starts living his own life, he learns by living his own life. Yes, he is ready sometimes to commit mistakes; it is good to commit mistakes sometimes, that is the only way to learn. The man of knowledge never commits mistakes--but he has committed the greatest mistake, the mistake of always remaining borrowed.

And these men of knowledge are very dangerous, because they go on pouring their knowledge into each other. It is a strange phenomenon. When you feel too burdened you need somebody so that you can pour out your knowledge and feel a little unburdened.

I have heard:

A merchant went to a farmer to get a pound of butter. The farmer insisted on swapping the butter for a pair of woollen socks. When the merchant reported this to his wife, she said, "I'll unravel some wool from our bedspread and knit him a pair of socks." When it was finished, the pair of socks was exchanged for a pound of butter.

When the merchant needed more butter, his wife once again unravelled more of the bedspread and knit more socks, which were exchanged for butter. Finally, she had only enough wool for one sock. The merchant took the sock to the farmer and asked for a half pound of butter for it.

"Nothing doing," replied the farmer. "I give you a full pound. You see, I really don't wear the socks. My wife unravels the wool and uses it for knitting a bedspread, and there's just enough in this one sock to finish it."

That's how it goes on--this stupid society.
Avoid knowledge and plunge into learning.

The last question

Why am I so afraid of you?

IT IS A GOOD SIGN: the beginning of a relationship with me. It is natural to be afraid of me, because I am going to be a death to you. I am going to destroy you. Utterly. Only then can I help you. Only then can you have a new life, a new being, a new beginning.

So fear is natural. In spite of the fear, go on coming closer and closer to me. Don't listen to the fear. The fear is simply saying that whatsoever you have had up to now will be taken away: "Escape!" You have a certain amount of knowledge, it will be taken away. The fear is simply an indication from the head, a signal from the computer, saying, "Escape from this place. This man is dangerous, he can destroy your knowledge. And then you will have to learn from ABC, know well, and all that you have done up to now will be a sheer wastage. Listening to this man is dangerous--he will make you feel that all that you have is useless, and sooner or later you will have to renounce it. Before it happens, escape! Avoid this man!"

You have a certain character, a certain morality, and I am bent upon destroying it--because I don't believe in morality. I believe in consciousness, not in conscience; conscience is again borrowed, like knowledge. Consciousness is learning.

I would like you to live according to your consciousness. That is the good life for me, the true life, authentic, spontaneous. It never does any harm to anybody--it cannot. But the life of conscience is a bad life; even if you are moral, even if you go on doing good, you are only a do-gooder. And you harm. And you harm in such subtle ways that you are not aware, and neither do your victims ever become aware of what you have been doing to them.

I will take your morality. I will give you religion, but I will take your morality away--because for a moral person it is very difficult; to have the experience of religion is almost impossible for him. A moral person lives according to the society; he never rebels. And religion is only for those who are ready to rebel. A moral person lives only like a sheep, with the crowd; whatsoever the crowd says is right he says is right, and whatsoever the crowd says is wrong he says is wrong.

Just watch. Are you a part of the crowd? Or do you have some consciousness of your own too? If the crowd is going to destroy, you are ready to destroy. If the Hindu crowd is going to destroy a Mohammedan mosque you are ready to destroy it, because you are a Hindu and whatsoever the Hindu crowd is doing is right. If the Mohammedan crowd is going to kill Hindus you are ready to kill Hindus.

Down the ages, the so-called religious people have been such great murderers. They talk about love and they create hate and nothing else. They talk about peace and they create war. Look at the hypocrisy! They come with Bibles in their hands, but soon those Bibles turn into swords. Those Bibles are just facades-- behind is hiding the imperialist, the one who wants to dominate the whole world. In the name of God they are simply trying to impose their ego on the world. And then egos fight. It is not a question of the Hindu fighting the Mohammedan or the Christian fighting the Mohammedan, it is the fight of so many egos.

Watch: whenever a crowd is doing something, can you think on your own? Your religions are crowds, your nations ate crowds. If India is fighting China, then all Indians are with the Indian government, right or wrong--it is the motherland, right or wrong. And all Chinese are with the Chinese government, right or wrong.

Nobody thinks on their own.

My whole approach is to make you conscious of what you are doing, how you are doing it. Are you being just a coward and a sheep and a follower in the crowd? Or are you thinking on your own? I will take away all your mob-psychologies. Fear arises, because that is where you have always belonged. Suddenly you will be left alone. If you are not a Christian you will not know who you are. Great fear shakes you, quakes you. If you are not a Catholic who are you? If you are not an Indian then you lose your identity. A great crisis of identity arises in you--that is the fear.

And you are always afraid of truth--because you live through lies, and when truth arises you start seeing your lies. It becomes difficult, it becomes almost impossible to carry them any more; you have to drop them. But you have invested your whole life in them.

A wealthy landowner burst into his home one day and, in a

voice filled with despair, cried to his startled wife, "Marushka, there is a terrible rumour in town--the Messiah is coming!"

"So what's terrible?" asked the wife. "I think it's wonderful! Why are you frightened?"

"I have good reason to be afraid," he whimpered. "We have a fine dairy herd, a barn full of grain, and our orchards are laden with fruit. Now we will have to give up everything and follow Him!"

"Compose yourself," said the wife soothingly. "The Lord our God is good. He knows how much suffering we Jews have had to endure. We had a Pharaoh, a Haman--always somebody; but our dear Lord got rid of them all. Just have faith, my dear husband. He will get rid of the Messiah also!"

It creates great fear if you hear the Messiah has come. Then what about all the investments that you have made? And you will have to give up everything and follow him. Who wants a Messiah to come? People always like the idea that he will come some day, but not today--some day far away, distant, then they can tolerate the idea that he will come.

That's why when Christ declared: "I am the Messiah you have been waiting for!" the Jews could not trust him. They said, "You can't be. He will come, certainly, but you are not that."

And there is logic in it. The logic is: people only wait for the Messiah, they don't really want him to come. Waiting is good, it makes one feel good--"I am religious and I am waiting for the Messiah. And when he comes I am going to renounce everything." And deep down one hopes that he will never come. He has not come up to now; he will never come. On the surface one pretends that he will come, deep down one knows that he will never come. And one thing is always there: even if he comes we can always say, "You are not the Messiah."

They had been waiting for centuries, and when Jesus declared, "I am the Messiah," they were angry. This man was destroying their whole game of waiting. Waiting is so beautiful; nothing ever changes, one goes on waiting and one goes on doing whatsoever one wants to do. And suddenly this man comes and he says, "I am the Messiah--now follow me. Come, follow me!"

And they are afraid. Their crops are ready and their orchards are full of fruit. "Is this the time for the Messiah to come? And the business is going so good..." And one is chasing a woman and he is just on the right track and it is only a few days time and she will be his--and this is the time for the Messiah to come? "Come and follow me"? Can't you wait a little?

Great fear arises. Out of that fear they killed Jesus. Just to defend themselves they killed Jesus--just to defend their fruits which were ripe, and the woman who was just going to be in their hand, and the man who was just going to succeed. This was not the right time for the Messiah to come. It is never the right time.

A Messiah is acceptable in the future, always in the future, never in the present--or in the past, but never in the present. The Jews had to deny Jesus. They said, "He will come, but you are not the Messiah." Christians say he was the Messiah, but now he is in the past, now there is no fear.

I am saying to you: I am the Messiah herenow. It creates fear, it creates great anguish and anxiety: "So what to do? And the fruits are ripe, and success is just within reach. And this man has come to disturb all, and he says, 'Come, follow me.'"

That's why you are afraid. Everybody is afraid. Remember always, the courageous person is not one who has no fear--no, there exists no man like that, who has no fear. The courageous man is one who goes in spite of the fear. He feels the fear, but the pull of love is greater than the pull of the fear. He chooses love rather than the fear.

The courageous man is also afraid. Don't think that only you are afraid; everybody is afraid, it is natural. And don't wait for the time when there will be no fear, and then you will follow! That time will never come. You have to follow in spite of the fear. And if you follow, soon you will see, the deeper you move into love, the energy that was involved in the fear is released from the fear and becomes love energy.

And when all fear is transformed into love, that fire is sannyas, that fire is disciplehood. That fire purifies one. Passing through that fire of love, one becomes pure gold.

THE SECRET OF THE
DROWNED MAN

More frail and illusory
Than numbers written on water,
Our seeking from the Buddha
Felicity in the after-world.

Already, over the heart
Not a cloud is hanging,
And no mountain is there
For the moon to hide behind.

In our way through this world
Of birth and death,
We have no companion;
Lonely we die,
Alone we are born.

The vast flood
Rolls onward
But yield yourself,
And it floats you upon it.

Who sees naught,
Says naught,
Hears naught,
Simply surpasses
The Buddha.

THE THINKER IS CREATIVE WITH HIS THOUGHTS. This is one of the most fundamental truths to be understood. All that you experience is your creation. First you create it, then you experience it, and then you are caught in the experience--because you don't know that the source of all exists in you.

There is a famous parable:

Once a man was travelling, accidentally he entered paradise. In the Indian concept of paradise there are wish-fulfilling trees there, *kalpatarus*. You just sit underneath them, desire anything, and immediately it is fulfilled--there is no gap between the desire and its fulfillment.

There is no gap between a thought and a thing. You think, and immediately it becomes a thing; the thought realizes automatically. These *kalpatarus* are nothing but symbolic for the mind. Mind is creative, creative with its thoughts.

The man was tired, so he fell asleep under a *kalpataru*, a wish-fulfilling tree. When he woke up he was feeling very hungry, so he simply said, "I am feeling so hungry, I wish I could get some food from somewhere." And immediately food appeared out of nowhere--just floating in the air, delicious food.

He was so hungry that he didn't pay much attention to where it had come from--when you are hungry you are not philosophic. He immediately started eating, and the food was so delicious that he was caught up in the food. Once his hunger was gone he looked around. Now that he was feeling very satisfied, another thought arose in him: "If only I could get something to drink..."--And there is still no prohibition in paradise; immediately, precious wine appeared.

Drinking the wine relaxedly in the cool breeze of paradise under the shade of the tree, he started wondering, "What is the matter? What is happening? Have I fallen into a dream, or are some ghosts around and playing tricks with me?"

And ghosts appeared. And they were ferocious, horrible, nauseating. And he started trembling, and a thought arose in him: "Now I am sure to be killed. These people are going to kill me."

And he was killed.

This parable is an ancient parable, of immense significance. It portrays your whole life. Your mind is the wish-fulfilling tree, *kalpataru*--whatsoever you think, sooner or later it is fulfilled. Sometimes the gap is such that you have completely forgotten that you had desired it in the first place; sometimes the gap is of years, or sometimes of lives. So you can't connect the source.

But if you watch deeply you will find all your thoughts are creating you and your life. They create your hell, they create your heaven. They create your misery, they create your joy. They create the negative, they create the positive. Both are illusory--the pain and pleasure, the sweet dream and the nightmare, both are illusory.

What is meant by calling these things illusory? The only meaning is that they are your creation. You are creating a magic world around yourself--that's what is meant by the word *maya*. Everybody here is a magician. And everybody is spinning and weaving a magic world around himself, and then is caught--the spider itself is caught in its own web.

There is nobody torturing you except yourself. There is nobody except yourself; your whole life is your work, your creation.

Buddhism insists on this fact very emphatically. Once this is understood, things start changing. Then you can play around; then you can change your hell into heaven--it is just a question of painting it from a different vision. Or if you are too much in love with misery you can create as much as you want, to your heart's content. But then you are never complaining, because you know that it is your creation, it is your painting, you cannot make anybody feel responsible for it. Then the whole responsibility is yours.

Then a new possibility arises: you can drop creating the world, you can stop creating it. There is no need to create heaven and hell, there is no need to create at all. The creator can relax, retire.

That retirement of the mind is meditation. You have seen all, this way and that. You have enjoyed and you have suffered, and you have seen the agonies and the ecstasies: love and hate, anger and compassion, failure and success, you have seen all. Ups and highs, lows and downs, you have lived all. Slowly slowly, this experience makes you alert that you are the creator.

If you have been on any drug trip, you know it. The drug simply releases your mind energy and things start happening. You are transported into other worlds. If a person suffers from paranoia and he goes on an LSD trip, the trip is going to be very very horrible. He will be persecuted, he will be surrounded by enemies, he will suffer much. If the person is not living out of fear but living out of love and joy, he will have beautiful experiences.

Aldous Huxley says that he lived great heavenly experiences through LSD. But Karl Reiner says that he went through hell. And both are right. They think they are against each other, criticizing each other. Reiner thinks drugs create hell. Drugs create nothing. All that is created is by your mind; drugs can only magnify it. They can exaggerate, they can allow things to appear in a very magnified form, a thousandfold bigger than they are. Molehills are turned into mountains, that's all. The drug can only exaggerate, but the seed is supplied by your mind.

Your whole life is a kind of drug trip. When you are under the impact of a drug, things happen fast; immediately; they start happening. When you are living the usual ordinary life, things take a little longer time, conventional time. But it is the same trip. Your life and your drug experiences are not separate, because both are out of the mind--how can they be separate?

Buddhism says: To see this point is to allow an awakening in yourself. Then both can disappear. You can simply let things disappear by not cooperating, by withdrawing yourself, by becoming a simple witness, watching.

Scientists say that every day in twenty-four hours, fifty thousand thoughts pass through the average man. Fifty thousand thoughts are continuously passing. You don't allow all the thoughts to be realized; you choose. There are good thoughts, there are bad thoughts, there are beautiful thoughts and there are ugly thoughts--you choose.

It is almost as if you have a radio and all stations are available on the radio. The whole noise of the world and the politicians is available on the radio. But you choose the station--that choice is yours. Or you can choose not to put the radio on; you can choose to put it off. Then all that noise disappears.

Exactly this is the situation. A meditator chooses not to choose any station; he simply puts the radio off or disconnects it. And all the noise and all the politicians and all that nonsense disappears.

But if you want to choose, you can choose; you can choose any station. People become addicted to stations. When you enter into somebody's room you can see his radio. You will see the needle on the station to which he is addicted, whether the radio is on or not. Slowly slowly, the radio remains always fixed on that station which he likes.

That is the situation of your mind. When I look into you I see your needles fixed. Somebody has decided to live in hell; his needle is fixed. And it has remained fixed for so long that now even to change to another station is going to be difficult. It has gathered rust; maybe it has lost the capacity to be moved from here to there, it may have become fixed. You may have left it there for many many lives; you have forgotten that other stations are available. And you think you are suffering, you have to listen to this noise. You don't like it at all, but what can you do?--you have to listen to it.

People become addicted to their thoughts. Then that thought comes more often, is repeated more, creates a groove in the head, in the brain cells, and becomes your reality. Naturally, you think what can you do?--you are a helpless victim.

Buddhism says: You are not a victim at all--not a victim of fate, not a victim of God, not a victim of the so-called theory of karma. These are just tricks, strategies, to avoid seeing the fundamental law of life.

When you are suffering you try to find some explanations. There are beautiful explanations available. Somebody says, "This is how God wants it to be, so what can you do? You have to live it. It is not in your hands. Man is impotent and God is omnipotent. What can you do? All that is possible for you is either to suffer happily or to suffer unhappily. Suffering is going to be there, so just suffer--as happily as possible, as ungrudgingly as possible, without complaint. Suffer with acceptance--that's all that you can do. Or you can go on crying and weeping, but nothing can change it. It is beyond you."

This explanation helps people. Then they remain fixed in their groove. They forget that they can change anything.

Buddhism declares that man is free. That is Buddhism's greatest contribution to human consciousness and the history of human consciousness, that man is utterly free, that man is freedom. There is no God who is programming you, there is no programming at all. You are programming yourself; you are a self-programmer.

There are other explanations: those who don't believe in God, they believe in karma. You are suffering, you are in anguish, and you say, "What can I do? It is my past life's karma, I have to go through it." This helps acceptance; it is a consolation. It gives you a certain kind of rest, it makes life a little easier--otherwise it will be too difficult, it will be impossible, it will be unbearable.

Once you see the point that it is predetermined in some way or other--whether by God or karma, it is the same strategy, with no difference; karma is another God, only words are different--now nothing can be done. You have done something wrong in the past life, there is no way to undo it now; the only way is to go through it. Go through the worst, and hope for the best. Remain in a kind of consolation that something good will come out sooner or later.

This is why people are in so much misery--because of their explanations! If you have explained your misery, how are you going to transform it? If you have a certain explanation that helps you to accept it as it is, then there is no possibility of transformation.

Buddhism wants to take away all theories and consolations. Those are all tranquillizers, deadly poisonous. And the insight that Buddhism wants to share with you is that you are the sole agent, the sole creator of your life; nothing else determines it. Each moment you are in control. You just have to see it and you have to try a few changes--those changes will help you to become more aware.

One day you are feeling very miserable: just sit silently in the chair, relax, and start enjoying. Just do the opposite--don't get into the trap of the misery: start smiling. In the beginning it will look false. Just get euphoric, blissed out. Start swaying, as if there is a great dancing energy in you. And you will be surprised that, slowly slowly, that which had started almost like a pretension is becoming real. The misery is disappearing; it no more has its hold on you, something has changed. A laughter is arising in you.

Your old habit will say, "What are you doing? What about karma? This is not supposed to be; you should not do such things. This is against all philosophy and metaphysics. Go back into the old groove! This is not right, you are cheating--you have to be miserable when there is misery. This is inauthentic, this is pseudo."

The mind will bring in all kinds of things to create the disturbance again. But insist: "This time I am going to drop out of the theory of karma. I am going to jump out of the wheel! This time I am going to choose the polar opposite." Start dancing, singing, and see, and you will be surprised. But you will have experienced a great truth, that it changes; that the climate changes, that the clouds disappear, that it becomes sunny, that you are different.

Sometimes you are feeling very happy: do the opposite, become miserable--for no reason at all, just become miserable. In the beginning it will again be just acting. But soon you will get into the act--because all that you are doing is nothing but an act, so it can be changed.

What you call your authentic life is also just an act. Maybe you have practised it long, that's all, but it is an act. So it can be changed for another act. And once you have learnt the trick of changing your acts from one to another, you will be able to see your freedom. You are something beyond the acts.

The function of a master is to destroy all your acts and to make you capable of being free. Buddhism says you are free, utterly free. Experience your freedom, and slowly slowly get out of the old ruts.

It happened, a professor of English language was invited to speak on the philosophy of life. He was a retired professor, well-known, but he wanted to make a little change in the title of the lecture. He said, "Let it be called 'The grammar of life'." A professor of English language: the people who had invited him thought, "It is right, it is the same--the philosophy of life or the grammar of life."

And do you know what the professor said when he spoke? He said: "Live in the active voice, not the passive. Think more about what you make happen than what happens to you. Live in the indicative mood, rather than the subjunctive. Be concerned with things as they are, rather than as they might be. Live in the present tense, facing the duty at hand without regret for the past or worry for the future. Live in the first person, criticizing yourself rather than finding fault with others. Live in the singular number, caring more for the approval of your own conscience than for the applause of the crowd. And if you want a verb to conjugate, you cannot do better than to take the verb 'to love'."

This is his grammar of life. His whole life he must have been teaching grammar, grammar and grammar. Now it has become almost an unconscious habit; he cannot think in any other terms.

This is how you are caught, you are caught by habits. There is no karma that is holding you--or if there is any karma it is nothing but your habits. The thing that you have been doing again and again, becomes almost a determining factor in your life, becomes decisive.

But one can drop any habit. You may have been smoking for thirty years--but you can drop this cigarette, half-smoked, on the floor and never take another cigarette in your hand. You are free. If you cannot drop it, that simply means you are choosing not to drop it. If people say, "How can we get out of misery?" they are simply saying, "We don't want to get out of misery." They are deceiving themselves.

People come to me and they go on asking, "How to get out of this?" And I am simply puzzled, because only they are holding themselves in it; nobody else is there. They can come out of it just as easily. The energy that they are putting into being in it is more; less energy is needed to come out of it. But they have forgotten one thing--they have forgotten their freedom.

The message of Buddhism is freedom. Freedom from God, freedom from heaven and hell, freedom from fear, freedom from the future--freedom from all these explanations that man has created down the ages and is burdened with and crushed by.

I have heard:

An efficiency expert died and was being carried to his grave by six pall-bearers. As they approached their destination the lid of the

coffin popped open and the efficiency expert sat up and shouted,
"If you'd put this thing on wheels you could lay off four men!"

Just the whole life's habit--an efficiency expert is an efficiency
expert. And don't laugh at it, this is what you are doing. You are
living in habits, you will die in habits. And because of these habits
you will miss real life. Real life consists of freedom. And once you
know that you are free then there is no obsession to choose this or
that. You can choose not to choose.
That state is called Buddhahood.

More frail and illusory
Than numbers written on water,
Our seeking from the Buddha
Felicity in the after-world.

THIS IS AN IMPORTANT SUTRA. Go slowly into it. The first
thing: to ask the Buddha to help us is foolish, for three reasons.
First, he cannot. Second, even if he could he would not. Third, we
do not need to be helped since we are all Buddhas already.
Zen people say: Because of these three reasons, to ask for
help from the Buddha is foolish. First, he cannot. Why can he not
help? Because from his standpoint you don't need any help at all.
From his standpoint your whole situation is ridiculous. Your whole
misery is false! Rather than being kind to you, he would like to
laugh at you--although he does not laugh. He goes on showing his
kindness to you, just not to offend you unnecessarily.
But the basic thing is, from the standpoint of a Buddha all your
misery is so stupid. It is as if you are in a house which is on fire--
doors are open, windows are open, you can jump out from
anywhere, and you are just sitting there and shouting, "Help me!
How am I to get out of this house? My house is on fire! Bring me
maps, guidebooks; teach me techniques, methods, to get out."

And the house is on fire and you are just standing in the middle of it. And the doors are open and the windows are open--you can get out immediately, not even a moment has to be lost. The whole situation is ridiculous.

A Buddha knows that you are all Buddhas. The day a man becomes enlightened, for him the whole world becomes enlightened. Then he can see through and through: he can see your eternity, he can see your eternal purity, he can see hidden inside you the source, the God. And you are crying, and weeping, and he can see your treasure and your empire. And you are begging, begging for help.

The Buddha cannot help you, because he can see your misery is self-created, illusory. And he cannot help you for another reason too: the master himself has disappeared as an ego, as a self There is nobody who is inside; a Buddha is pure emptiness. Who is there to help you?

You can take all the help that you need, but nobody is there to help you. Let it be very clear: you can partake of the energy of a Buddha, you can eat as much of his energy as possible, you can drink him and you can become intoxicated with him--but he cannot do anything on his own. The door exists no more.

A Buddha is simply an availability. The master remains available in *satsanga*; his presence, or his absence, is there. You can take in as much as you want, you can allow that presence to penetrate you as deeply as you open your heart. But all depends on you. Yes, you can help yourself through the Buddha, but the Buddha cannot help you. There is no activity possible on the part of Buddha.

Sometimes when you come to me and ask, "Osho, will you help me?" you create a problem for me. If I say I will, I am false. If I say I will not, you are hurt--I am unkind, unloving. The situation is: I am available. You can help yourself through my presence; I cannot do anything.

The master is a catalytic agent. His presence can trigger a

process in you, but he cannot be a doer. He cannot take any initiative, he cannot be a manipulator, he cannot impose any discipline or character on you, he cannot force you to change--all that violence is gone. Violence is a shadow of the ego; the day the ego disappears, all violence disappears.

That's why I say a do-gooder is not a good man. And the man who is after you and is trying to change you is not the man to be with. The man who is hankering to change you is an egoist, he wants to make you according to his ideas. He is dangerous, he will destroy you; he will not be helpful to you. He will cut from you this part and that part, he will change things in you. He has a blueprint with him, he has a certain idea that has to be implemented. He will not be bothered about you. His whole concern is with his idea; you are just a plaything.

That's what your so-called mahatmas go on doing. They go on giving you patterns of life, they go on forcing things upon you: "Do this, don't do that. If you do this you will be rewarded, if you don't do this you will be rewarded. If you obey, the paradise is yours. If you disobey, then you fall into hell."

These people are dangerous people. These are politicians, not religious people at all. Their whole effort is to change people; they enjoy it. But people are not things. A man is not a canvas, you cannot paint him the way you want. The man is God, the woman is God, each person is divine. Who can change a person? Just the very idea of changing a person is sacrilegious, is a sin.

Many people come to me and they say, "Why don't you give discipline to your sannyasins?" Who am I to give discipline to my sannyasins? I am available. Whatsoever they want, they can have; that is their choice and their freedom. I am here to teach a single thing: Freedom. No interference in it. If they choose to remain in the world, fine. If they choose to get out of it, fine. With me, all is good. But the greatest value is freedom.

A Buddha cannot be asked to help you. He is help--but a passive help, just a presence, a door. You can pass through it, but the door cannot drag you through itself. Be aware of the fact: if you are with a real master he will not drag you anywhere. He will shower his presence on you, he will remain available in a thousand and one ways, but he will give you freedom to choose, freedom to be. His presence is not active, cannot be; all action is violent. His presence is passive. So, for three reasons, it is not possible.

Ikkyu says:

More frail and illusory
Than numbers written on water,
Our seeking from the Buddha
Felicity in the after-world.

Secondly, he would not help you, because anything that is given to you from the outside cannot become your eternal nature. Even a Buddha cannot give you the truth--because truth is not a thing to be given or taken, it is an experience that arises in you. The Buddha is an occasion where you can bloom. But nothing can be given to you, nothing can be transferred.

There are things which are untransferrable. They only arise; they grow. They are not commodities, they grow like a fragrance grows in a flower.

Truth is your fragrance. So even if he wants, a Buddha would not help you--because anything given from the outside, just because it has been given from the outside, becomes untrue. It is no more the real gift. The real gift has to arise in you, it has to be given birth by you, through you. At the most, the master can be a midwife.

That's what Socrates says he is--a midwife. The child grows in the womb of the mother: the midwife can become an occasion to bring the child out of the womb more comfortably, conveniently. That is the function of a master.

God is growing in your womb. The master can be an occasion

to bring this birth to happen in comfort, with as little pain as possible, with as much joy as possible, with celebration.

Thirdly, he cannot help, because he sees we do not need any help. All that we need is an awareness of our freedom, an awareness of the fundamental law that thought creates reality--that we are creators, that each and everyone is a creator.

Never think for a single moment that God has created the world. You have created your world. And there is not one world, there are as many worlds as there are people here. You live in your world, your wife lives in hers. That's why the clash--those two worlds are continuously clashing. They have to clash, they are overlapping.

You like one thing, your woman likes another thing. There is no way to convince each other, this way or that--a liking is a liking. You would like to go to this picture, to this movie; she wants to go to some other picture, to some other movie--a liking is a liking. Two worlds together, overlapping, interfering with each other--hence the conflict. We don't live in one world. There are as many worlds as there are people.

And the Buddha is one who has seen the truth of it, that he is the creator of his world, and he has retired from it. He creates no more. A Buddha lives here in the world, without a world. That's the meaning of being a Buddha: he lives in the world but there is no world for him. He lives in the world but the world is not in him. His own creation has completely disappeared. His canvas is vacant: he creates no more, he no more projects any dreams.

To come close to a Buddha means coming close to an emptiness. Hence the fear. One feels scared. If you look into the eyes of a Buddha you will feel utter emptiness, an abyss. And you feel as if, if you fall into it, you will never reach to any bottom. There is none. There is no bottom, it is eternal emptiness one falls and falls and falls. One disappears but never comes to the bottom of it.

The Buddha cannot help you, because he sees your dreams. It is as if you are asleep and you are seeing a very dangerous dream. A tiger is following you and you are screaming, and in your sleep you shout, "Help! Help!" And somebody is sitting by you side awake. What do you think he is supposed to do? Should he try to help you? Then he will be just as stupid as you are. Then he will be as asleep as you are, or even more.

He will laugh. He knows there is no tiger; it is your creation, it is your imagination. He may have a good laugh. But you are suffering--you tiger may be imaginary, but for the moment your suffering seems to be true. Tears are coming, you are shaking and trembling.

What should the man do who is awake? He cannot save you from the tiger, because there is no tiger in the first place. But he can do one thing: he can help you to be awake.

That's why these sutras are so depressing, you feel sad. Pradeepa has written a letter to me; her brother and her brother's wife are here and she has written, "Osho, the last time they were here you were talking about Sufis, and they were thrilled by the talks--that's why they have come again. And now these Ikkyu sutras: they are sad and they create sadness." She has asked me to do something so that her brother and brother's wife don't feel sad here. Nothing; can be done. With Ikkyu, I am Ikkyu.

But this sadness is of immense value. And you are not here just to be entertained, you are here to be enlightened. There is nothing wrong in being entertained--if you decide to be that, fine--but then you missed a great opportunity. You need to be enlightened. And before one becomes awake one has to pass through many sad layers of one's being. Layers upon layers are there of sadness that you have repressed--because you never wanted to be sad, you have never faced it.

Buddha brings all your sadness in front of you, because his commitment is not to your sleep and your dreams. Maybe those dreams sometimes are sweet, but a dream is a dream, whether sweet or bitter. Even if it is very entertaining it is a dream, and the time is wasted.

Truth may not be very entertaining, but it is enlightening. And once you have seen the truth, life moves into a totally new dimension. That dimension is of blissfulness. And remember again, blissfulness does not mean happiness--because what you mean by happiness is again entertainment. What you mean by happiness is nothing but pleasure, sensation, thrill.

Blissfulness has the quality of peace in it, silence, stillness, undisturbedness. There is no pain and no pleasure: that state of non-duality, Buddha is interested in it. And to attain to it, if one has to pass through sadness it is worth it. Any cost is okay, because what you are going to realize is beyond all values; it is beyond all your comprehension.

The Buddha Way is the way of awakening. But you can be awake only when your sadness is emphasized totally. Otherwise who would like to be awake? You have to be made alert about your sadness, about your hell. You have to be made aware of your death, of your illness. You have to be made aware of all the agonies that you have passed through and you are passing through and you will have to pass through. This whole thing has to be emphasized.

I have heard:

A Broadway producer decided he was fed up with the extravagant ballyhoo in the advertising of so many shows. He decided that he would insert a clause in his contract giving him the right to approve all advertising for the new play he was producing.

Writer after writer prepared ads embodying the honesty and sincerity he said he wanted in his ads. He turned them all down. Finally, one brought in a piece of copy which read like this:

"Here is a play which combines the drama of Shakespeare, the wit of Rostand, the strength of Tennessee Williams, the intellect of Marlowe, and the plot mystery of Dickens. Greater than Hamlet, more moving than the Bible, this is a play destined to live for ever."

"That's it!" shouted the producer. "No exaggeration! Just the simple truth!"

You are living in an exaggerated kind of hope, it can be destroyed only by an exaggerated kind of sadness. The opposite polarity has to be brought in. You are hiding all your wounds, Buddha would like to open them all up. Naturally, one does not like it. Seeing one's wounds, it hurts. Life starts looking very very painful, one feels lethargic about living. Then what is the point? One starts thinking of committing suicide.

That's the point Buddha would like you to reach. Where you start thinking of suicide, only there is sannyas possible--not before it. When you think the whole life is meaningless, only then does your energy start being concentrated on one point--that now some other meaning has to be searched for. "This life has failed, in toto. Now another life has to be searched for. I have lived outside myself and seen it is all sadness and agony. Now I have to turn inwards--a one-hundred-and-eighty-degree turn."

That's why these sutras appear so sad. They bring the truth of your life into focus.

More frail and illusory
Than numbers written on water,
Our seeking from the Buddha
Felicity in the after-world.

AND PEOPLE ARE SO STUPID that even when they come to a Buddha--who knows no future, who knows no past, who lives in the eternal moment--they still ask about the after-life. They want to have some felicity in the after-world. They are not interested in being awakened herenow, they are interested in making some beautiful world after death.

Buddha is interested absolutely in the herenow. He wants you to be awake herenow. But you go to him and ask, "Is the soul immortal? Will I live after death? What will happen after death? What happens after death? Where do people go?

And Buddha used to laugh at all these questions and he would simply put them all aside. In fact this was his usual way: whenever he would enter a town his disciples would go around the town declaring to each and everybody, "Don't ask these eleven questions." And these eleven questions were all questions of metaphysics: the afterlife, God, heaven, hell, karma--all that kind of garbage.

Buddha used to say: Just ask about the immediate, that which is the question right now. Let me become the answer for that.

People don't want to ask that, they want to avoid it. You are in misery and you ask, "What will happen after death?" People come to me too; they say, "What will happen after death?" I say, "First see what is happening before death." They are not interested in that. Before death? Who bothers about before death? The real question is after death.

If you can't see what is happening now, and you don't want to see it, the story is going to be the same later on too. Somebody has asked, "This question has been pursuing me from my very childhood: how does the stone feel inside? Inside the stone, how is it?"

Inquire first how it feels when you are a man--because once you were a stone too, but then you were worried, I know, then you were worried about how it feels to be a man. Now you are a man, you are worried about how it feels to be a stone. Are you going to miss all the opportunities?

And remember, it feels the same. If you can know how it feels inside right now, you will know how it feels inside anywhere else. The inside is the same, only outsides differ. One is a woman from the outside, another is a man from the outside; from the inside, nobody is a man and nobody is a woman. And the man is continuously puzzled by the woman. Even your greatest men, so-called greatest men, are continuously puzzled by the mystery of the woman.

How does it feel? From the inside it is the same, even in a stone. The inside is always the same; only the outer periphery, the shape and the form, is different. Inside is God. God is the inside of all things.

But these questions! Now, just think, a person has been continuously thinking since childhood--it must have become an obsession--how it feels inside a stone. And the person has not yet asked, "How does it feel right now inside me?"

Buddha is interested in the immediate, the imminent. Go into the right-here-now: enter your reality and see. And whatsoever you will know will solve all your problems. No metaphysics is needed, meditation alone is enough.

But people used to ask him, "Help us for the future life." And he was ready here, available here, to transform you. But you are not interested in being transformed here, because you have a thousand other things to do. You are thinking that after life is finished and all the beautiful things of life have been done, then resting in the grave, yes, then one can meditate. Then one can think about great things. Why be bothered right now? Right now there are so many things to do--so many interesting things to do.

Buddha cannot help you for the future, because for a Buddha there is no future. The only time for a Buddha is the present. He cannot help you for the past, because there is no past. It is all one now.

Already, over the heart
Not a cloud is hanging,
And no mountain is there
For the moon to hide behind.

And if you can see it, and if you can go into the right-now of things inside yourself this moment, you will be surprised...

Already, over the heart
Not a cloud is hanging,
And no mountain is there
For the moon to hide behind.

All is clear there! This very moment! Just you are not there. All

is clear there--just clarity, transparency, crystal clarity. And it has
been so since time began. Your inner purity is absolute, it cannot
be contaminated.

It is just as if a man is asleep, you shake him and he awakes.
Even while he was asleep his capacity to awake was not
destroyed. It was there; it was like a substratum. On the top maybe
there was a layer of sleep, of dreams, but deep down he was
awake. Otherwise how can you wake him just by shaking him?
Just an alarm, just somebody calling from the outside, and he
opens his eyes and asks, "Who is calling me?" And he was asleep
and he was dreaming a thousand and one things, and he was
utterly lost in those things. But something was still aware.

That something is always aware. That something never loses
its awareness.

You are lost in thoughts; thoughts are dreams. You are lost in
the head--and that clarity exists in the heart. The head is your
confusion, naturally: fifty thousand thoughts passing through your
head every day, it is really always rush hour, twenty-four hours.
And these fifty thousand thoughts I am talking about are for the
very very normal average man. I am saying nothing about the
neurotics and the philosophers and the thinkers, mad people; I am
not saying anything about them, this is just average.

So many thoughts passing through the head: how can you
remain clear? So many clouds: how can you see the sun?

But there is a space inside you, a fountain of clarity: your heart.
Slip out of the head and fall into the heart. And suddenly one is aware.

Already, over the heart
Not a cloud is hanging...

Because not a single thought ever passes through the heart.
The mechanism of thought is in the head, and the mechanism of
awareness is in the heart. The heart is always aware. That's why
whenever you do something from your heart it has a beauty, a

transcendental beauty, a grace. It has something of the divine--
maybe a small thing, a small gesture, but in that gesture God is
revealed. And whatsoever you do from your head is always
calculated, cunning, clever, and remains profane and ugly.

Already, over the heart
Not a cloud is hanging,
And no mountain is there
For the moon to hide behind.

There it is all clear. And both these spaces are available to you,
but somehow you are just standing by the roadside, surrounded by
the traffic and the noise.

Get out of your head and get into your heart. Think less, feel
more. Don't be too much attached to thoughts; get deeper into
sensations. Just see the change: it is only a change of gestalt. You
are lost in your thoughts, you cannot hear the birds singing. Then
you change the gestalt. Just the focus changes, it is a shift. You
are no more worried by the thoughts: suddenly all the birds are
there singing, the flowers blooming, the sunrays passing through
the trees and the wind playing around with the old dead leaves.
Just a shift...

And exactly that has to be done. Hence, one who really wants
to be awakened needs to learn all the ways of sensitivity. Feel
more, touch more, see more, hear more, taste more. And your
mahatmas have all dulled your sensitivities. They have been telling
you, "Don't taste, taste is dangerous." They have been telling you,
"Don't listen to music; forget your senses." And because you have
become closed to all your senses, your feeling has disappeared--
because feeling can live only through the nourishment that your
senses give it.

So when a new person comes here and sees people hugging
each other, holding hands, dancing, singing, he is puzzled--because
he knows only one kind of ashram, the cemetery kind, where people

are dead, just sitting under the trees, dull, not feeling anything, just chanting "Rama-Rama-Rama". And that chanting is just a kind of lullaby so that they can force all their senses to fall asleep.

If you want to be aware, you have to be sensitive. You have to allow all your senses to become aflame. Then the heart starts living. Then the lotus of the heart opens and there is never any confusion.

In our way through this world
Of birth and death,
We have no companion;
Lonely we die,
Alone we are born.

DON'T GET LOST too much in the world of relationship, because all relationship is dreaming. Remember your utter aloneness.

Lonely we die,
Alone we are born.

And this life is just an overnight's stay. Don't become too much committed to it, don't get too much involved. Staying overnight in a *sarai*, you don't get involved. You remain there for the night and you know that in the morning you have to go, so you don't become worried about the caravan *sarai*.

This life is just a journey, this life is only a bridge. Pass through it; don't become too much involved in it. Remain aloof, detached. And that aloofness and that detachedness has not to be a forced thing. If it is forced, you have missed the point. It has to be out of your understanding. If it is forced, it will kill your senses; if it is out of understanding, your senses will become more alive.

The vast flood

Rolls onward
But yield yourself;
And it floats you upon it.

And remember, if you are not involved then there is no question of fighting, no question of struggle. It is the involved people who become very very struggling, because they have certain ideas of what has to be done. They want the world to be in a certain way; it has to be changed. They become so involved that they cannot sleep. They have to paint the walls of the caravan *sarai*, they have to decorate the walls, they have to change the bed, they have to arrange the furniture--and by the morning they have to go. And the whole night is lost in arranging and fighting and changing things.

Out of understanding, not out of enforced practising, you start floating with life. Then all is okay; then you don't push the river...

The vast flood
Rolls onward
But yield yourself;
And it floats you upon it.

And if you start fighting with it you are simply fighting with yourself and with nobody else. If you start struggling with life you will become more and more closed, naturally, in defence. If you start struggling with life you will be defeated, because you will dissipate your energy in fighting.

If you don't fight with life, you float with the flow, you go with the river, you go downstream--you don't try to go upstream, you have no ideas, you are simply in a kind of surrender with life--this is trust, this is surrender. And this is it! Then a miracle happens: if you don't fight with life, life simply helps you--it takes you on its shoulders.

Have you seen any dead body floating in the river? And have you watched the secret of the dead man? When he was alive he was drowned by the river, naturally. Maybe he didn't know how to fight, he didn't know how to swim: he was drowned by the river. He must have been fighting, he must have tried hard to get out of it: he was drowned.

Now he is dead, and he is floating on the surface. What has happened? It seems when he was alive he didn't know the secret. Now he knows; now the river is not drowning him. The best swimmer is one who knows how to behave with the river as if you are dead--as if you are dead--then the river takes you.

This is let-go: living as if dead, living with no attachment, living with no possessiveness, living with no clinging. Living with joy.

Who sees naught,
Says naught,
Hears naught,
Simply surpasses
The Buddha.

And if you can float with the river without making a house on it, this miracle will happen:

Who sees naught...

You will be able to see that which cannot be seen. And you will be able to see that when it happens, the seer also disappears. You will be able to see that which cannot be called the seen.

This is the trinity of experience: the knower, the known and the knowledge. This is the trinity of experience. If one becomes totally relaxed, this trinity disappears. Then there is no one who is a knower and then there is no one who is known; there is simply knowing. The knower and the known have dissolved into knowing. All nouns have dissolved into the verbs of life.

Who sees naught,
Says naught...

THERE IS AN EXPERIENCE which is not an experience, which you cannot call an experience. That's why Buddha never talks about God--because to talk about God is wrong, is to falsify, is to belie, is to betray. It is something that nobody has never seen. It is something that is seen only when the seer has disappeared, it is something that comes to your vision only when you are not there. It is utter unity: there is no division of the experience and the experienced, of the observed and the observer. All distinctions, all dualities, have disappeared. How can you say anything about it?

Says naught...

That's why the sage says a thousand and one things about a thousand and one things, but never says anything about the truth. Nothing can be said about it. The sage is the truth. You can partake of him, you can drink as much as you want out of him, you can live in his vicinity and you can be transformed by being close to him--but there is nothing which can be said about truth.

The Tao that can be said is not the true Tao. The truth that is uttered becomes immediately a lie.

Who sees naught,
Says naught,
Hears naught,
Simply surpasses
The Buddha.

Buddhahood is the absolute transcendence of all--even Buddha is included in that all. One becomes a Buddha only when he surpasses even Buddhahood. Try to see it. It somebody says "I have attained Buddhahood" and clings to it as an experience, he has not yet attained; it is still a part of the world of experience. The ego still persists--maybe it has become very subtle, but it is there.

The real Buddha is one who has disappeared--disappeared as

an experiencer. That is the utter surpassing. And in that surpassing, one is God.

The God to which we have become very much accustomed is our own imagination; it is not the true God. The God of the Christians and the Hindus and the Buddhists is not the true God. The true God is the God about whom never a single word has been uttered. The God of the Bible and the Vedas and the Koran is not the true God. The true God is one about whom there has always remained utter silence. Our Gods are our creations.

I have heard:

A woman in Manhattan died and willed her estate to God. To settle the estate a case was filed, naming God as a party thereto. A summons was issued and the court went through the motions of trying to serve it. The final report stated: "After due and diligent search, God cannot be found in the City of New York."

But that is the kind of God people are searching for. What kind of God are you searching for? You have a certain image in your mind, that he will be playing on the flute, he will be like Krishna, or he will be just a magnified form of Jesus Christ, or he will be like this or like that...You are simply going through the empty gestures of religion; the real religion has not possessed your life yet.

The real God cannot be imagined; the real God happens only when all imagination has ceased to he. The real God cannot be seen; the real God can be seen only when the seer is no more. The real God cannot become an object--to reduce God to an object is to destroy him, is to kill him, is to murder him. The real God always happens as the innermost core of your subjectivity--not there, but here. Not then, but now. Not out, but in. And that 'in' also is only for a moment--once God has happened, that 'in' also disappears. Then there is nothing outer, nothing inner: all is one.

This is the function of a master--to make you alert of that which cannot be said, of that which cannot be described. A great love is needed, a great sympathy is needed towards the master. Only then these unimaginable things, indescribable things, indefinable things, can be understood.

The master cannot give you God, but he can make your heart aflame with a longing for him.

The young salesman was perturbed. He had lost an important sale he had thought was in the bag. While discussing the matter with his supervisor, the salesman shrugged his shoulders and said, "You can lead a horse to water but you can't make him drink."

"For Pete's sake!" shouted the supervisor. "Who told you to make him drink? Your job was to make him thirsty!"

That is the job of a master--to make you thirsty for something invisible. It is a mad kind of thirst, you cannot logically prove anything about it. It is a kind of infection. Hence *satsanga* is needed--you have to be in deep communion with the master. Slowly slowly, something contagious enters your being. The look of the master's eye, a gesture caught in a moment when you were utterly silent and the traffic of the mind was no more moving--just a pause, a silence, a period...and something starts stirring in you.

The master is there outside you. His very presence starts calling forth something that has been asleep for long. One starts arising, one opens one's eyes.

It is a very strange relationship to be with a master, the strangest--because the master is not, and the disciple is too much. And, slowly slowly, the nothingness of the master overwhelms the disciple: seeing the beauty of nothingness, he starts dropping his somebodiness.

It is related that a fire broke out in a house. Within, a man was sleeping. They tried to carry him out through the window, but could not. The man was heavy, big, weighty. They tried through the door, but could not. He was really fast asleep.

And you know, when a man is fast asleep he becomes very heavy; if he is awake you can carry him easily. Have you observed the fact? Just carry a small child when he is awake, and he is light. And carry the same child when he is fast asleep, and he is heavy. Sleep has a quality of heaviness in it--maybe sleep is more in tune with the gravitation of the earth, awareness is more in tune with the levitation of the sky. These words are not used in a scientific way, just metaphorically, but whenever a person becomes awake he becomes very light. And if you have carried somebody who is in a coma then you will know, it becomes almost impossible to carry him.

They tried from the window, they could not. They tried through the door, they could not.

One wise man said, "Wake him up, he'll get out by himself!"

That's what the purpose of a master is. By his awareness, by the impact of his awareness, your sleeping quality slowly slowly is dissipated, dispersed. His light provokes your light, his silence calls forth your silence.

And remember, the master is not doing anything in particular. He is just being here: it all happens of its own accord. But the disciple has to be very watchful, the disciple has to be very very attentive, the disciple has to be very very focussed and concentrated. The disciple has to remain with unblinking eyes. The disciple has to be almost in a kind of deep infatuation, all alert--just as when you are in love, the whole world disappears, only your beloved is.

Unless the master is your beloved, your lover, unless your whole energy is moving towards him, transformation will not be possible. You have to watch every gesture, every nuance.

After Billroth, the Viennese surgeon, had told his students that a doctor needed two gifts--freedom from nausea and power of observation--he dipped his fingers into a bitterly nauseating fluid and licked it off, requesting them to do the same. They did it without flinching. With a grin, Billroth said, "You have passed the first test well, but not the second, for none of you noticed that I dipped my first finger in, but licked the second."

Yes, one has to be very very attentive with a master to see every gesture, because in those gestures is the real message. The way he walks, the way he sits, the way he looks at you, the way he is. What he says is secondary. What he *is* is primary, very fundamental. So those who are lost in their arguments and in their words and in their theories, in their expectations, go on missing.

More frail and illusory
Than numbers written on water,
Our seeking from the Buddha
Felicity in the after-world.

Already, over the heart
Not a cloud is hanging,
And no mountain is there
For the moon to hide behind.

In our way through this world
Of birth and death,
We have no companion;
Lonely we die,
Alone we are born.

The vast flood
Rolls onward
But yield yourself,
And it floats you upon it.

Who sees naught,
Says naught,

Hears naught,
Simply surpasses
The Buddha.

Surpass the Buddha! I am bent upon it here, I mean it! Surpass
the Buddha--because that is the true Buddhahood when you have
surpassed even the Buddha.

That eternal source is available to you. You are fortunate. Don't
miss it.

BUDDHAS
WITH CLOSED EYES

What is the difference between
waiting for Godot and waiting for God?

The idea of being a master,
sitting there doing nothing,
appeals to me.
What do you say?

I feel I'm drowning.
I feel suffocated.
Help me!

What is this ego?

Please can I be simply normal?

I only want to sit in your lap!

The first question

What is the difference between waiting for Godot and waiting for God?

NO DIFFERENCE AT ALL. All waiting is waiting for Godot, because all waiting is in vain. You cannot wait for God, because God has already arrived. God is already the case; God is not in the future. God is just this, all this: how can you wait for it?

If you wait for it you miss it. Waiting for God is a way of escaping from God, a very tricky and cunning way, very clever and subtle--so subtle that one can deceive oneself through it. What do you mean when you say 'waiting for God'? God is not there, far away, distant. You are not to travel to God, there is going to be no pilgrimage. God is where you are; you are because of God. God is in your breathing, God is your life. There is no other God than life.

To avoid life, people have created images of God--they are not images of God, they are escapes from God. People are avoiding God, hence they have made temples and mosques and gurudwaras and churches. These are not made by religious people, remember, these are made by the irreligious. Those who don't want to get involved with God, those who want to postpone it, they have created the temples and the so-called religions. Those religions give you a feeling that God will be in the future--in some

other country, in some other land, in some other space, in some
other world, but never here. And he is here.

And he is here in the songs of the birds and the green of the
trees and the red of the trees and the gold of the trees. He is in the
bird on the wing...he is everywhere. You need not even go outside
yourself to find him. He is your innermost core, your substratum,
your very being. How can you wait for him? It will be just like a fish
in the ocean waiting for the ocean; it will be utterly foolish.

So all waiting is for Godot. All waiting is futile. Wait, and you are
wasting. Wait, and you are avoiding the guest who has already
come--he is knocking on the door in the wind, in the rain, in the
sun; he wants to enter into you. And you are doing your prayer in a
shrine, secluded. Or you are sitting in your cave waiting for God.
Who are you trying to deceive? You don't want to receive the guest
right now: be truthful. You are afraid to receive the guest; it may
disturb your whole pattern of life. It is certainly going to disturb
your whole pattern of life.

To receive God means a death, a disappearance--because the
two cannot exist together, you and God.

Martin Buber, one of the great thinkers of this century, says the
relationship between man and God is that of I-thou. It is not--
because there is no I and no thou. It is not a relationship at all,
because relationship needs at least two.

God is when there are not two. When you are not then
something becomes clear which has always been there, but
because of you--the turmoil that you are, the anguish that you are,
the nightmare that you are--because of you it was impossible to
see it. You are the dust in the eyes; you are the darkness around
yourself God is available but you are not available to God. You
cannot wait for God; God is waiting for you.

But why do people go on thinking in terms of waiting? It gives
great illusions: some day it is going to happen. Just see the
working of the mind, the functioning of the mind. The mind is
always a seeker, always desiring something or other; it exists

through desire and seeking. Sometimes it seeks money, sometimes it seeks meditation, but there is no basic difference. It is the same game--played with different words but not a bit has changed, played with beautiful names but the same game.

Somebody is seeking power here, and somebody is seeking power there--power there in the other world--and he calls it 'God'. Somebody wants to be special here, and somebody else wants to be special there. The disciples of Jesus ask him again and again, "We know that you will be exactly on the right side of God, you will be on his right hand. But amongst your disciples, who will be next to you there in that other world, in that kingdom of God? Who will be next to you?"

What is this desire? The same power politics, the same hierarchy, the same ego trip.

The mind remains a seeker. The mind cannot exist with fulfillment, it can exist only in hunger. Mind can only exist in a state of starvation. If you are utterly fulfilled and there is no hunger and no starvation and you are contented, mind disappears like dewdrops in the morning sun--you will never find the mind again.

Mind looks in the future, searches in the future. And when you are focussed in the future--some goal, faraway goal... And the farther the goal is, the better for the mind--because if the goal is not very far, then sooner or later you will achieve it.

God, the idea of God, is the best goal for the mind. The worldly man does not have such a great idea, because his ideas are not impossible, they are feasible. He wants to make a little bigger house--it is not such a big deal, it can be done. It will be done; one day he will have the bigger house--and then? Then the mind has to create a new desire again.

Just see: why does the mind have to create new desires? Booauoo your old dooiro hac boon fulfillod, and mind can exist only in desiring. You have so much money, and mind wants to double it. Then one day you have doubled it: now what to do? Mind has come to a point where suicide is automatically going to happen. If the mind wants to live again, again a new desire has to be released, projected: again you want to double the money, and so on and so forth.

The worldly man has to change his desires many times, again and again; he has to constantly renew his desiring. And who is this other-worldly man, the so-called religious--the saint, the mahatma? He is more cunning. From the very beginning he has chosen something; he is waiting for the impossible. It is not going to happen, it has never happened, because it has already happened. There is no way for it to happen, it is impossible. He can live on and on--this life, another life, and another life--and his goal is so utterly impossible that he will not need to change it. He has a permanent goal.

The worldly man has temporary goals, not very very distant. The worldly man thinks in instalments: one desire, then another desire, a better car, a better house, a more beautiful woman...

The other-worldly man has chosen the ultimate in desire. God is the ultimate in desire--not the true God, the God of your idea is the ultimate in desire. It is intrinsically impossible. You can go on waiting and you can go on striving, you can go on seeking.

To see it, that seeking is the way of the mind, that seeking is mind, that seeking is the source of all tensions and anguish and anxiety, is to become aware of a great phenomenon. Then you don't start seeking God, because that is seeking again. Then all seeking simply disappears, withers away. In the knowing of the fact that seeking creates mind and mind is anguish, seeking disappears. And with the seeking disappears the shadow, the mind.

And when there is no seeking how can there be waiting? When there is no desire how can there be waiting? When there is no desire, no seeking, there is no waiting. Suddenly you are here and now. You cannot move a single inch, you cannot go anywhere, there is nowhere to go now.

In that immediacy, God becomes available. It is better to say that you become available to God--God has always been available from his side.

It is as if the sun has risen in the morning and you are sitting in your room with closed doors and windows, in darkness. Open the doors, you become available to the sun. The sun was already available--just the meeting happens.

You cannot wait for God. All waiting is for Godot. Godot means the one who never comes, who cannot come, whose arrival is impossible. And the only impossible thing is that which has already happened--how can it happen again? You are alive, and you are waiting for life, Now, this is ridiculous.

The real man of religion does not think in terms of God. He thinks in terms of life or, even better, of living--because life can again become an abstract idea. Living, moment-to-moment living. In that very living, one knows what God is, because one knows who one is.

Your idea of God is an escape from living. You are afraid of life, of love, you are afraid of death. You are afraid of ten thousand things, and they are there and you don't want to see them eye-to-eye. You don't want to know what exactly the case is. How to avoid it? You become engaged somewhere else. You create a great desire in your mind, a distant desire--somewhere in the future it will be fulfilled--and you become obsessed with it. Then you worship God, and you are worshipping a false God.

All worship is false, because real worship consists of living, not of worship. Real worship consists of small things. Not that you do rituals--all rituals are just strategies to create a belief that you are doing something special, something sacred. You are simply being stupid, nothing else. You can decorate your stupidity--you can chant Vedas and you can read Bibles and you can make great rituals in the churches and temples and you can sit around a fire and chant great songs--but you are simply being stupid; this is not being religious at all.

But a religious man lives day-to-day, moment-to-moment. Cleaning the floor, and there is worship. Preparing food for the husband, and there is worship. Taking a bath, and there is worship. Worship is a quality--it has nothing to do with the act itself, it is the attitude that you bring to the act. If you love the man and you are preparing food for him it is worship, because the man is divine.

Love makes everyone divine, love reveals the divinity. Then it is not just your husband, it is God in the form of your husband. Or it is in your wife in the form of a woman--but it is God, ultimately God and always God. A child, your child: God has come in a certain form to you.

Recognize! See! And there is worship. You may be just playing with your child and it is worship--far more significant than what you do in the temples; the worship in the temples is just plastic.

Real life has to be lived in an authentic sincere way, with totality, with joy, with celebration. And then you can forget all about God--because each moment you will be meeting him, each moment you will be coming across him. Then everything is just a manifestation of God. God is the prior condition of everything-- nothing can exist without him. So only he exists, and all else is just a form.

A wave, a tidal wave arises, or a small ripple, but both are the ocean. The small ripple is as much the ocean as the tidal wave. A Buddha walks, he may be a tidal wave. And then an ordinary man, the man who comes to mend your shoes, is also God--maybe a ripple, but no ripple is any less the ocean. There is no question of being less or more--a ripple is as oceanic as the tidal wave, and the smallest particle is as divine as the greatest mountain. There is no question, because God is not a question of quantity, it is a question of quality.

Anything that is alive is divine. This vision is religion.

So, Chinmaya, no waiting is waiting for God. All waiting is for Godot. Don't wait--you have waited long enough. Can't you see the futility of waiting? Accept my invitation to live God! Don't wait. Waiting is not the way, living is the way. Live God! Start this moment! What else do you need?

I am here, you are here, the trees are here, the birds are singing and the vast sky is surrounding you. What else do you need? What more do you think there will ever be? Nothing is going to be added to it and nothing is going to be taken away from it; this totality will remain as it is.

I am existing in the same totality in which you are existing. But I am existing with open eyes and you are existing with closed eyes-- that's the difference, the only difference; not much.

You are Buddhas with closed eyes.

And it is just a question of a decision to open your eyes. You have the capacity to open them--because if you can close them you can open them. The very possibility of closing them is there because you can also open them. It is your decision, it is your choice.

You have chosen to live without God because you are afraid of God. And then you say, "I am waiting for God." Very tricky. You don't even want to accept the truth, that you have been escaping from God. So you create false Gods--ikons and idols and temples- -and you go there and you do stupid things there and you call them yagnas, prayer, and all that stuff.

See that you have been escaping. This hurts--because seeing it, your whole mind topples down to dust. Your whole life is based on this strategy to go on escaping, to go on postponing. "Tomorrow I will live"--that is your way of living. Tomorrow, never this moment. Next life, after death, in some other time, in some other world...

There is no other world. This is the only world there is. And all those paradises and heavens are just your imagination, to escape, to get involved--dreams to avoid reality.

My whole process consists in bringing you to this moment. Just this--and God showers on you and God arises in you. And the God within meets the God without, and then there is great joy.

In short, stop being a seeker! Now, Chinmaya is a seeker, hence the question. Stop being a seeker! People enjoy these ideas very much: "I am a seeker of truth" or "I am seeking God." And then they look at you with that bullshit of holier-than-thou, a seeker of truth, a seeker of God. But seeking is basically wrong. Seeking is wrong--what you are seeking is irrelevant.

Don't be a seeker. You have been a seeker for many many lives. It is time! Wake up from your seeking and start living! When are you going to live if you go on seeking and seeking and seeking?

Start living. Eat when hungry, and while eating be utterly there in it, and it becomes worship. Fall asleep when tired, but really fall asleep totally. And if no dreams pass, that is total sleep; it is worship. If sleep is without dreams it has the quality of meditation. That's why Patanjali says that *samadhi* and *sushupti*--the ultimate state of ecstasy, and deep dreamless sleep--are very similar. Why similar? Because in deep sleep dreams disappear, thinking disappears. So is the case in samadhi: all thinking disappears, all imagination disappears, all dreaming disappears. The only difference is, in deep sleep you are unconscious, in samadhi you are conscious. Otherwise both take you to the same home, to the source.

Sleep totally. When you are walking, walk totally, let everything else disappear. Enjoy the totalness of a morning walk, all that is involved in it--the children playing and the dogs barking and the birds on the wing and the clouds in the sky, and you there. What more can you ask for? What more joy? If you can't be happy with such a beautiful world, with so much continuously being given to you, where do you think you will be happy?

Walking, just walk. Listening, just listen. Talking, just talk. Be totally in it--then each act is transformed, becomes luminous. This is the way to live God.

I don't teach you any seeking for God, I teach you living God. Living starts this moment. Seeking of course has to start tomorrow, always tomorrow. And the tomorrow never comes.

The second question

I want to be a master. The idea of just sitting there and doing nothing appeals to me very much. What do you say about it?

GREAT IDEA! SOME IDEA! But it is very difficult to just sit. You are so restless. If you can just sit, you are a master! But think of just sitting, doing nothing--can you allow that much rest to yourself even for a single moment?

That's what I go on telling you: Sit silently, passively, doing nothing, just being. And you look at me with bewildered eyes: "Just sitting, doing nothing?" People ask me, "Can't we chant a mantra? Please give us a mantra, so we can at least chant a mantra when we are sitting." That mantra is for nothing but your restlessness.

Maharishi Mahesh Yogi's transcendental meditation has appeal in America because America is so restless. People can't sit silently; they have to do something or other. If there is nothing to do then they have to repeat Rama-Rama-Rama or Coca-Cola-Coca-Cola-Coca-Cola--but something. Coca Cola is a great mantra: repeat it and you will have all the benefits of transcendental meditation.

What happens when you repeat a mantra? It just gives your restlessness something to do. It becomes concentrated, then you can sit. But this is not real sitting; you have escaped again. Now you have escaped into the mantra. A mantra is a mind trip. Just sitting means no mantra, no thought, no movement. Just sitting exactly means just sitting.

Yes, then you can become a master; you have become a master. People will start coming to you of their own accord-- because whenever somebody just sits, such grace arises in that non-moving energy because he is utterly in the present. He can't move anywhere--he can't move to the past, he can't move to the future. He is just utterly here, he is totally one with this moment. In that, he is bridged with reality, he is one with God.

And a man who is one with God is a master. In that moment, such great gravitation arises in him that people will be attracted, people will start moving towards him. He may be sitting deep in a cave in the Himalayas and people will start reaching there, people will start finding the way to where he is. There is some unconscious pull.

In Buddha's days there was no way, because the world was really very disconnected. Nations existed secluded; there was nothing like newspapers, radio, television--no way to spread the message. But people started moving. From almost every nook and corner of the known world, people came to Buddha. Somehow it functions, it spreads; it has its own momentum.

You will be a master if you can sit silently. But the very idea of being a master will not allow you to sit silently. You will open your eyes to see whether disciples have started to come or not: "And what am I doing here? It is time, and nobody has come--I don't see any photographers and any newspaper people and media people coming..." You will not be able to sit silently. You will start waiting for disciples: that's the meaning of the desire to be a master.

A master is one who has no desires. Now, even the desire to be a master is enough; it won't allow you to be a master. A master is not trying to be a master--he is. He is not managing it, it is spontaneous. He is not searching and seeking for disciples; they come. It happens on its own. The very silent energy of a master-- that luminous energy of being alert, peaceful, at ease, at rest, at home--starts many people moving towards that source. It is not really in the mind that it happens, this pull. It happens deeper than the mind: it happens in your unconscious.

You say: I want to be a master.

That will be a barrier. And the reason is the idea of just sitting there and doing nothing. You must be a mighty lazy person. Just sitting there and doing nothing is not a state of laziness, mind you.

It is of utter energy, ultimate energy. It is not a kind of sleep, a kind of coma; it is not lethargy. It is a reservoir of energy. The energy is not moving anywhere, the energy is accumulating. And the more it accumulates, the more powerful it becomes.

You must be just a lazy person. The idea appeals to you, because to be a disciple seems to be difficult, arduous--you have to do this and you have to do that, and you have to meditate, and you have to pass through so many things, and here is Yoga and Zen and Tantra and Sufism and you have to find and search and roam and wander and inquire, and it seems to you to be a long journey. You would like to simply be a master.

I have heard:

A poor half-wit was befriended by a millionaire lover of music who happened to have a private orchestra. One day the half-wit came to his benefactor and asked for a position in his orchestra. Astonished, the rich man said, "I had no idea you could play an instrument."

"I can't," was the answer. "But I see you have a man there who does nothing but wave a stick around while the others play. His job I can handle."

That job is not easy, that is the hardest of all--from the outside it appears to be very easy.

Just sitting is the hardest thing in the world, the most arduous thing in the world. You can do everything--you can go to Everest and you can go to the moon--but just sitting? that is impossible. You can move into any kind of activity--that fits, that fits with the ego, that enhances the ego: you become a great doer.

But when you are sitting and doing nothing, what happens? What is the difficulty? The greatest difficulty is, when you are not doing anything you start disappearing--because man exists through his acts.

Jean Paul Sartre is right when he says that man defines

himself through his activity. You are what you do.

You are a doctor because you do a certain kind of work. You are a painter because you paint, you are a singer because you sing. Your identity is given by your action. You are this, you are that--your definition comes from your activities. When you are not doing anything who will you be? A doctor, a painter, an engineer, a singer--who? You will be nobody. You will be simply nobody! Your identity will start disappearing, your definition will slip out of your being. You will be utterly nude and naked and not knowing who you are.

And that is the arduousness of it--it is very arduous. You will be getting into a great chaos, and great fear will arise in you: what is happening? You will immediately rush into some act, you will start doing something. And once you start doing something you are again at ease, because again you know who you are.

Have you not watched it? Just sitting silently in your room, have you not observed it again and again that you start doing something meaningless? People start moving their furniture, arranging the paintings again or cleaning the books or the cupboard--they have to do something. Because when they are doing, they are perfectly settled in their knowledge of who they are.

You are a housewife: doing something, you know. You are a mother: when the child is with you, you know who you are. You are a husband: with the wife you know who you are. When the wife dies, something in the husband dies immediately, because he becomes very much frightened--now who is he? He had become accustomed to living with the idea that he is a husband.

Mulla Nasrudin's wife died and he was crying like anything. One of his closest friends could not believe his eyes--such big tears were coming from Mulla's eyes, and he had never seen the man cry. And he had always thought that this man is a brave man-- just crying like a child?

To console him the friend said, "Don't be worried, Nasrudin,

time heals everything. Within three to six months you will have
forgotten this woman. And I say to you, you are still young enough-
-you will fall in love again, you will be married again. So don't
become so desperate."

Mulla looked with anger at the friend and he said, "What are
you talking about? Six months? And what am I going to do
tonight?"

If you have become accustomed to a wife, she has become
part of your definition. In the night, alone, you will be afraid--afraid
of the fact that again your definition has disappeared.

When a very rich man goes bankrupt what happens? Why do
people commit suicide when they go bankrupt? Is money so
valuable, more valuable than life? The problem is, that was their
definition. Now there is no money in the bank, their soul has
disappeared, they don't know who they are. And it seems so
arduous to define themselves again, to start from ABC, to start
begging again. And it will take thirty or forty years to be able to
make that much money again and have that definition again. That
seems to be too long and too much; it is better to disappear, it is
better to drop the whole effort.

Your activity keeps you defined; it gives you a certainty, a
security. Whenever you are not doing anything you become
uncertain. An abyss starts yawning in your being and you feel you
are falling into the abyss, and immediately you jump to do
something.

I have seen people reading the same newspaper again! I used
to travel for fifteen years continuously--almost three weeks a
month I was travelling and watching people. Sometimes it would
happen that only one more passenger was with me in the
compartment, and I would watch him He would read the same
newspaper again and again--and would feel a little ashamed also,
because I was there. He would open the window and close the
window, open the suitcase and arrange it and close it again--and

he would become very much ashamed also, because somebody was just sitting there and doing nothing. And he could not sit. And he would try to sleep, and he could not sleep, and he would jump up and go to the bathroom and come back. And he was not an insane person, just a normal person, for twenty-four hours caged in a compartment, not knowing what to do.

Have you not seen people?--their holidays are the most difficult days; they don't know what to do. The whole week they think that Sunday is coming and they are going to rest, and they never rest on Sunday! They start a thousand and one things: they start mowing the lawn or they start fixing things around the house. They get more tired on Sunday than they ever get in their office--because in the office who works? One simply postpones. Files move from one table to another table--they go on moving and moving and moving, and nothing ever happens. People become so skillful at avoiding in the office, that is their work there. To avoid, to say no, not to do anything: that is their activity there.

Psychologists are perfectly aware that once a person becomes retired he dies earlier than he would have died if he had remained in his work. Ten years' difference happens. If a man was naturally going to live eighty years, and when he is sixty he becomes retired...And he had been hoping for that retirement his whole life--he was thinking, "Just a few years more and I will get retired and then I will rest and do all those things that I always wanted to do. I will read great poetry,.listen to great music, play the guitar or make a beautiful garden, or go to the mountains and rest in the sun, in the wind..."

And when he becomes retired all that happens is he simply becomes afraid of death--nothing else happens. Once he is retired he starts losing his identity. He was a collector or a commissioner or something, a prime minister, a president...

When politicians are in office they are very healthy. Once they lose their office they become ill; they die soon. Harnessed, they can live long. Unharnessed, they don't see what the point of living is. People start neglecting you, people start ignoring you, you become a nonentity. And not only for people do you become a nonentity, you become a nonentity for yourself--because you don't know now who you are. You had been a prime minister, now you are not a prime minister--then who are you? And no answer arises.

No, sitting silently is very difficult, just next to impossible-- unless you are ready to die in silence, unless you are ready to lose all identity, all ego. Yes, if you are ready to lose all identity, the master will arise in you. But you cannot become a master.

When you have disappeared, the master comes. It is always God who is the master. That's why in the East we call the master divine. The West cannot understand it, because the phenomenon has been very rarely happening there. The West knows bishops, priests, rabbis; it does not really know the phenomenon of a master, it is very rarely happening there. It knows prophets, visionaries, it knows preachers, priests--but very rarely, only once in a while, has the West come across a master.

And whenever the West has come across a master it has behaved very badly with the master. with Jesus it behaved in a very uncivilized way, because the phenomenon was very much unknown. If Jesus had been just a rabbi, everything would have been perfect. But he was a master. He had disappeared, God had appeared in him. Now God was speaking, now Jesus was not speaking.

And when God speaks, God speaks with great authority. When God speaks, God speaks in absolute terms. When God speaks, God speaks like a God. Jesus says, "I am the truth." This is God speaking. Not Jesus, not Joseph's son Jesus. Christ, not Jesus. It is God speaking: "I am the truth." NOW, no rabbi has ever said that--how can the Jews forgive this man? He seems to be very arrogant and egoistic.

Now, see the ridiculousness of it. Always, whenever ego disappears, God appears. And God speaks in such ways that it looks as if the man has become very egoistic: "I am the truth! I am

the way! And nobody reaches God unless he comes through me."
Just see these words: "I have come to liberate you. I and my
Father in heaven are one." Now, these statements cannot be
tolerated. This man seems to be neurotic, mad, a megalomaniac,
has lost all senses, is insane.

Still psychoanalysts go on calling Jesus insane. And it looks
insane, because who in his senses can say, "I am the way, I am
truth, and nobody ever reaches God unless he passes through
me"? Who in his senses can say such things?

Yes, he was not in his senses. He was not at all--how could he
be in his senses? God was speaking, he was just a mouthpiece.

A man becomes a master only when the man disappears. So if
you have the desire to be a master, that very desire will prevent
you.

Right now, become a disciple. Slowly slowly, the disciple
disappears and the master arrives. The first step towards
masterhood is disciplehood.

The third question

I feel as though I am drowning and am trying to hold on to
something. Nothing comes to my hand. I feel suffocated. Give me
something, Osho. It is heavy. I will die or go mad. Help me, please.

THE ONLY REAL HELP will be to help you to be utterly
drowned. And of that you are afraid. I am here to drown you! not to
save you from drowning--because only those who are totally
drowned are saved.

You ask: I feel as though I am drowning...

Something great is going to happen: allow it! be drowned! What
is there to save? What have you got to lose? You have known only

miseries; you are a bundle of miseries and dreams and hopes and frustrations and expectations--you are a bundle of all these things. Let this bundle be drowned! Why are you worried? Why do you want to be saved? And if you are saved, this bundle will be saved.

No--because I love you, I cannot save you. Because I love you, I will help in every way so that you can disappear.

I feel as though I am drowning and am trying to hold on to something.

There is nothing that you can hold on to. You can imagine--and people when they are in desperate need do go on imagining.

My work here consists of taking all those imaginations away from you, slowly slowly, one by one. All toys have to be destroyed, so one day you can see the fact that there is nothing to hold on to. Only then will you relax and allow this drowning. Only then will you relax and die.

And after that death is resurrection.

Vedanta, go down. And don't try to hold on to anything, because there is nothing to hold on to.

Nothing comes to my hand...

Because there is nothing. Nothing can come.

I feel suffocated.

I know. I have passed through the suffocation myself--I can understand your misery, I can understand your helplessness. But I can't give you my hand, because if I give you my hand you will remain the same. I have to leave you as you are. I have to just sit on the bank and see you drowning.

Of course you will feel angry at me.

I have heard: A Sufi master was sitting on the bank of a river, and a man was drowning. And the man started shouting, yelling, "What are you doing there? I am drowning and I don't know swimming! Come and save me!"

And the master laughed and he said, "I don't know swimming myself, but I am not yelling. So what? If you don't know swimming, you don't know swimming! I don't know it myself, but I am not yelling. There is no need to yell."

Looks very hard--the story looks very cruel. But this is not an actual case, it is just metaphorical. This is the situation! Vedanta is drowning there and he is shouting for help and yelling, and I say to him: Don't shout and don't yell. Simply disappear. Relax and let go. Don't try to hold on to anything. This is the last struggle of the ego to be saved. This is the death that brings samadhi.

Nothing comes to my hand.

Yes, nothing is going to come. I am not here to supply you new toys, new supports, new props.

I feel suffocated.

I know. Don't try to save yourself, otherwise you will be simply prolonging your misery. Die. One has to learn the art of dying--and that is the whole art of disciplehood.

Give me something, Osho.

I cannot give you anything. I can only take things away from you. I have to make you absolutely nude, utterly empty.

That's what Ikkyu's sutras are saying again and again: the Buddha cannot help. All help will be wrong help, because through help your wrong life will be supported.

Give me something, Osho. It is heavy. I will die or go mad.

You cannot die, that much is certain--because nobody has ever died. You cannot die, because death is impossible. Death never happens. It is all life--life only goes on changing forms.

When a child is born out of the mother's womb the child thinks "I am going to die"--naturally. For nine months the child has lived in a certain way and now that whole way is being disturbed. How can he think that this is going to be a new life? The child thinks "this is going to be death."

You are in exactly the same situation. Now you are being taken away from a womb--the womb of the society, the womb of religions, the womb of concepts, abstractions, philosophies. I am taking you away from the womb in which you have lived up to now. It is hard, heavy. And the child thinks, passing out through the mother's womb, that he is going to die. Birth seems to be like death.

And again, when you really die one day--old, aged, and you die--do you think it is death? It is again a beginning of a new birth. Each death is a beginning of a new birth, and each birth looks in the beginning as if it is death. But it is all life. Life goes on changing its forms, from one form to another. The form dies and life jumps into another form.

Life is a flame that lives eternally.

You cannot die, don't be worried about it--because nobody has ever died. Death is a myth.

You say: I will die or go mad.

You cannot die, one thing, because death does not happen. And you cannot go mad, because you are already mad. Now there is no more to it. Man as he exists ordinarily is mad. What more madness can happen to you?

Just sit silently in your room for one hour and write down whatsoever comes into your mind; just write down whatsoever comes, with no editing. Just go on writing whatsoever comes--relevant, irrelevant, consistent, inconsistent, absurd, nonsense, rubbish--just go on. And you will be surprised: after one hour, when you look at it you will think "Has some madman written it, or what?"

We keep our mind repressed. We are afraid--if we look into it, it is mad.

I have heard: A woman was playing on the harmonium and singing. And her voice was so ugly, nauseating, that the neighbour could not sleep--and it was getting late, it was two o'clock in the morning. Then he knocked on her door and said, "Please stop now! Otherwise I will go mad."

The woman came out, opened the door and said, "What are you talking about? I stopped one hour ago!"

The man has already gone mad!

As man is, he is already mad. You cannot go mad--don't be afraid about madness. If you allow this death you will become sane for the first time. Ego is mad, ego is madness. And the ego is afraid to die--the ego is crying for help.

And you have fallen into very dangerous company, Vedanta. Here, no help is given, all helps have to be taken away. I remove, I go on removing all crutches. I know that if all crutches are removed you will be able to stand on your own, because you are not a cripple but the society has made you crippled. And the society has given you all kinds of crutches, and you have lived with those crutches so long that you cannot imagine yourself without them. Naturally, when you take crutches away from the crippled man he feels suffocated, he feels he is dying.

You are on the right track. Whenever this happens to anybody here I become very happy, because then I know the moment has come: if you can be courageous enough to go through this moment you will be reborn.

And you say: Help me, please.

Just the other day, Ikkyu's sutras were saying no help is possible, for three reasons. First, you don't need the help--in fact you have been harmed by all kinds of help that have been given to you. Nobody has allowed you to be on your own; so much help has been available to you--your mother, your father, your teachers, your priests. Even before the problem has arisen, answers have been fed to you, all kinds of help. This helping society, these advisers all around, they have been helping you--they don't bother whether you need it or not. They go on helping, they have a chronic obsession with helping. They are known as social servants: these are the most mischievous people in the world. Their mischief is such that you cannot see it: they help you, they give you good advice, they teach you character, morality and this and that--and they destroy your whole possibility of growth. They make you false, pseudo, they make you plastic.

When you fall into the hands of a master the process has to be reversed. All help has to be withdrawn. You are to be left in such deep aloneness that you have to grow, that you have to take the challenge of life. And in that very challenge the energy starts moving, starts taking a form, becomes integrated.

Have you not watched it? Whenever there is a difficulty and you face it, something in you becomes strong. Whenever there is a great challenge it gives you steel in your being. And this is the greatest challenge that you can come across--the challenge of a master, of being with a master.

You don't need help. Secondly, the master cannot enforce anything. He will not even enforce what is known as good, because enforcement makes everything wrong. You have to partake; the master is a kind of availability. You can take as much as you need, whatsoever you need, you can drink, you can eat, you can digest the master--but nothing can be done from the master's side in a very active way, no. He is a passive presence.

And whenever somebody is active he becomes violent. He starts crippling you; he starts watching everything, he becomes a kind of policeman. He starts interfering in everything: you should eat this, you should not eat that, you should go to bed at this time and you should get up at this time--he starts interfering with your life. He becomes totalitarian, he becomes dictatorial, he destroys your freedom. In the name of great values he cripples you, he paralyzes you.

The real master is just a presence. You can be benefitted, but it is up to you. He is available: you can take it or leave it, but nothing can be done actively from the master's side.

Thirdly, all that you are thinking is your trouble, your problem, your anxiety, is illusory. You have become very very clever at creating illusions for yourself. The basic illusion is the ego. And once that illusion is created then so many other illusions arise out of it.

Now, you are not dying--just the ego is dying. But you think "I am dying." If you can see it, how can you die? You were never born! Do you remember any moment when you were born? Have you any idea what birth is? If you were born then there must be some memory--you were not, and then suddenly you popped out--but do you remember? Those who have gone deepest into inner work have all said that you were never born. Birth has not happened, so how can you die? You are unborn, undying.

Ikkyu calls it 'the great medicine'. No help is needed. At the most you need an awakening--not help in particular, in detail, but just an awakening. For that, the master's presence is the alarm.

That's why I go on shouting at you continuously, whether you listen or not. I go on calling you. Some day, in spite of your sleep, in spite of you, you may listen. That very moment, you will open your eyes and all the nightmares that you were suffering from will disappear.

This drowning, this suffocation, is just a nightmare.

And remember that one becomes awake only when the nightmare reaches to its peak, never before. Have you observed or not?--sometimes in your sleep when you are passing through a great nightmare, a moment comes when the intensity of the nightmare, the very intensity of it, becomes a breakthrough: you are suddenly awake. Your sleep can tolerate only so much nightmare, it can settle and remain adjusted with only so much agony. Once the agony point reaches beyond the capacity of the sleep, sleep has to be broken--it will break on its own.

You are being followed by tigers and you are running and the terrain is rough, mountainous, and you are falling and bleeding and feeling more and more tired. It is an uphill task and the tigers are coming closer and closer and you can hear their roaring sounds and their approach is coming closer and closer and closer...and suddenly you are caught by those tigers. One has just jumped on your chest, is tearing you apart--and in that very moment the sleep disappears and your eyes open. You are perspiring, your heart is beating fast, the whole body is trembling, but there is no tiger; you are just holding your own pillow.

I am sitting by your side, fully awake, seeing the whole misery. Do you think I should feel compassionate? You are suffering very much, this tiger is going to kill you, so should I bring a revolver or do something? I will kill you if I bring a revolver--to kill the tiger you will have to be killed, because it is your dream; the tiger is not real. So I am amused. Sitting by your side I enjoy the whole journey that you are going through. I can see through and through and I know that sooner or later the tiger is going to get you--how long can you escape? You can escape from a real tiger, there is a possibility; but you cannot escape from an unreal tiger, there is no possibility. It is your creation--wherever you go it will follow you. It is your mind! How can you escape? Sooner or later you will get tired, weary. You will fall, you will slip from a rock and you will be caught by the tiger. And then tigers do what they know: the tiger will tear you apart.

And at that moment when the tiger is tearing you apart, sleep cannot continue; it is too much. The sleep is broken.

In fact that is the purpose of so many groups that I tell you to go through. Primal, Encounter, Samarpan--these are just to enhance your nightmares. You are seeing those nightmares, but very mildly; they never come to a peak, so the sleep continues. They have to be brought to a peak, they have to be brought to a climax--because only from the climax comes the change, the change of consciousness.

Vedanta, good. I am happy, I am pleased. Be drowned, with all my blessings, and the dream will disappear. And the disappearance of the dream is the only way to know that which is. The disappearance of the dream is the appearance of God.

The fourth question

What is this ego?

AN ANCIENT STORY:

A young woodpecker, who felt exceedingly vigorous one morning, looked around the forest and decided to start the day by pecking a huge oak. He had just gotten off to a good start when a bolt of lightning split the tree from top to bottom. The bird hustled out from under the debris, looked up at what was left of the tree, and murmured with a shudder, "My! I did not even know my own strength."

This is what ego is. It is a misinterpretation--what is already happening, you think you are doing it. Just a translation from happening to doing is the creation of the ego. Watch, and whenever you feel that you are doing something translate it to "It is happening." Read "It is happening" and the ego will disappear.

All is happening, nothing is being done. There is no doer and no 'do-ee', it is all happening.

The fifth question

Please can I be simply normal?

NORMAL IS OKAY, but what is *simply* normal? Again you are making a condition; you are making it complex. Simply normal? Is being normal not enough? What more is added by putting 'simply' in front of 'normal'?

The mind is such that it cannot be happy with the natural, the normal. It always makes conditions and through those conditions it falsifies everything. Normal is possible, but simply normal is not possible. That 'simple' will be something brought in from the outside.

Man has become so accustomed to the artificial that even when sometimes the desire to be natural arises in him, what he thinks about as nature is not nature, it is again his idea of nature. What he says is natural is again his idea of the natural--not the natural, because the natural needs no idea. You need not become natural, you are natural; just stop being artificial, that's all. No positive effort is needed to become natural--just don't try to be unnatural.

Do you follow me? A positive effort will always lead you into artificiality. Now if you ask "How to be natural?" you have asked a wrong question, you have started on the wrong track. And then somebody is bound to supply the answer--because wherever there is a demand, there is a supply. If you ask a wrong question you will find somebody to answer it--because people are so anxious to advise, to answer, to prove themselves wise, wiser than you. They are just hankering for somebody to ask the question. Ask, "How to be natural? How to be normal?" and somebody will show you the way. But there is no way to be natural; all ways lead to unnaturalness.

Drop all the ways, don't try to be anything. Forget about becoming, and then what is left is natural. The way to the natural is negative.

That's why Buddha's emphasis is on *via negativa*. He never talks about positivity. He always says, "No, no. Neither this nor that: *neti neti*." Just go on dropping.

But man has become really so unnatural that his idea of nature is also unnatural. Not only has man become unnatural, even animals who live with man become unnatural. Your dog starts learning from you and becomes unnatural, becomes diplomatic, political. He is feeling angry at you: you are not allowing him to sit in the drawing room where he wants to sit, because guests are coming. He is feeling angry. If he is natural he will jump at you. But he is just waving his tail, showing great love for you. Now you have created a split in the poor dog's mind. He is trying to be very polite to you, and really he wants to hurt you.

I have heard:

The story is told of an old lady who rented a furnished villa for the summer, and along with the villa went a large dog. In the sitting room of the villa there was a very comfortable armchair. The old lady liked this chair better than any others in the house. She always headed right for it.

However, much to her regret, she nearly always found the chair occupied by the large dog. Being afraid of the dog, she never dared bid it harshly to get out of the chair. Instead, she would go to the window and call, "Cats!" Then the dog would rush to the window and bark, and the old lady would slip into the vacant chair.

One day, the dog entered the room and found the old lady in possession of the chair. He strolled over to the window and, looking out, appeared very much excited and set up a tremendous barking. The old lady rose and hastened to the window to see what was the matter, and the dog quietly climbed into the chair.

Even animals become cunning, clever, calculating. In zoos, where animals have to live with other animals and in a human space, they start going neurotic, become mad, even sometimes commit murder or suicide too. This never happens in the natural state; no animal species kills its own kind, never. But in a zoo it happens. No animal goes mad in the natural state, but in a zoo it happens.

Man has become very unnatural. Don't ask me how to be natural, just watch how you have become unnatural. Watch each act, each gesture, and see the unnaturalness of it. And whenever you see that it is unnatural, that this is not true, authentic--that this is not coming from your being, that you are only pretending, that you are being a hypocrite--drop it!

Go on dropping. Slowly slowly you will see, all that was artificial has been dropped. Then suddenly one day nature is blooming in all its grandeur. You need not do anything for it--nature is that which cannot be brought. The unnatural is that which has to be brought. The unnatural needs a positive way, the natural needs no positive way. Just not being unnatural is enough for nature to take possession of you.

And the last question

* Beloved Osho, since I have been here, one feeling gets stronger and stronger--the only thing that I really want to do is sit on your lap.

USHA, JUST FAR OUT! But please don t start doing it. I have fifty thousand sannyasins: just think of me too, otherwise I will be killed in a stampede. But the idea is great, just as an idea--don't practise it.

The idea is symbolic: a great love is arising in you. It is good, it has to be so. Unless you are in deep love with me nothing is going to happen. Only through love, the transformation happens. And it is good that you have not projected it on me--otherwise, that too happens...

Just the other day, I read in the latest issue of Youth Times a statement of an Indian film actress, Pratima Bedi. She says, "Rajneesh is sexy." Now, I really enjoyed it! She came to see me once; she must have been there for four or five minutes in front of me. She says I was trying to hypnotize her and I was very sexy and the vibe was sexual.

If the monkey looks into the mirror the monkey cannot see the angel looking out of the mirror. This Pratima Bedi is a wonder-woman! But let me explain to you what a wonder-woman is. I came to know about the wonder-woman through Mulla Nasrudin. One day he was saying, "My wife, Osho, is a wonder-woman." I know his wife, I said, "What do you mean?" because I have never seen such an ugly woman before. "Wonder-woman?"

He said, "Yes, wonder-woman--because sometimes I wonder whether she is a woman or not."

And he also said, "There is only one word that can explain her: 'temperamental'." I said, "You puzzle me again--what do you mean?"

He said, "She is fifty percent temper and fifty percent mental.

Now, this Pratima Bedi--I cannot think of a more ugly duck. And she thinks I was being sexual with her. But something must have happened in her mind.

A mentally retarded man was accused of raping a young girl, so the police made him take part in an identity parade.

The poor victim was to be led into the room where she was supposed to pick out one of the ten men as her attacker, but as soon as she entered the room, the man pointed to her and said, "That's the one!"

It is good, Anand Usha, that you don't project it on me!

People go on projecting their minds. I am a mirror: you can see in me whatsoever you want to see. And when you see it, naturally you think it must belong to me. Nothing belongs to me. This man here, talking to you, sitting in front of you, is just empty. Nothing belongs to me--or, only nothing belongs to me.

You can see your faces, you can see your innermost instincts, you can see your unconscious, reflected in me. Remember always not to project it, otherwise that will be a misunderstanding. Your love is good: let this love go higher and higher--because always, almost always, it starts with the body. Nothing is wrong with the body, but that is the very very gross kind of love.

Be on your wings, move a little higher than the body, spread your wings in the sky. Leave the boundaries behind. Don't think that you would like to sit in my lap, think to meet me on higher altitudes--because I am there! If I am here in the body I am here just for your sake, a little while more. This body is just an excuse to be with you. I am almost cut off from it, just hanging around it a little bit, because I know many are in great need. And I am waiting for them, and they are coming.

But search for me on higher altitudes, move with me as high as possible. Then more and more clear vision will be available to you. At the highest peak, meet with me and that will be the meeting with God himself.

AN INVITATION TO EXPERIENCE

OSHO
Never Born
Never Died
Only Visited This
Planet Earth Between
Dec 11, 1931 - Jan 19, 1990

Osho is an enlightened Mystic.

During the course of thirty years of talks to seekers and friends, Osho would answer their questions, or comment on the teachings of the world's great sages and scriptures. His talks continue to bring fresh insight to everything, from the obscure Upanishads to the familiar sayings of Gurdjieff, from Ashtavakra to Zarathustra. Osho speaks with equal authority on the Hassids and the Sufis, the Bauls, Yoga, Tantra, Tao and Gautama the Buddha. And ultimately, Osho concentrates on transmitting the unique wisdom of Zen, because, He says, Zen is the one spiritual tradition whose approach to the inner life of human beings has weathered the test of time and is still relevant to contemporary humanity. Zen is another word for the original Hindi word Dhyana. In English you may translate it as 'meditation', but Osho says this is a poor translation. So call it Dhyana or Zen or whatever you may wish - Osho's emphasis is on *experiencing*.

Osho settled in Pune in 1974, and disciples and friends from all over the world gathered around Him to hear His talks and practice His meditation techniques for the modern man. Western therapeutic group processes, classes and trainings were gradually introduced so bridging the wisdom and understanding of the East with the scientific approach of the West. And now Osho Commune International has evolved into the world's largest centre for meditation and spiritual growth, and offers hundreds of different methods for exploring and experiencing the inner world.

Every year, thousands of seekers from all over the world come to celebrate and meditate together in Osho's buddhafield. The commune grounds are full of lush green gardens, pools and waterfalls, elegant snow-white swans and colourful peacocks, as well as beautiful buildings and pyramids. Such a peaceful and harmonious atmosphere makes it very easy to experience the inner silence in a joyful way.

For detailed information to participate in this Buddhafield contact:

OSHO COMMUNE INTERNATIONAL

17, KOREGAON PARK, PUNE-411001, MS, INDIA

PH: 020 628562 FAX: 020 624181

E-MAIL: commune@osho.net

INTERNET WEB SITE: http://www.osho.com